The Occasional History

of a Child Actress,

Tap Dancer,

Record Store Clerk,

Thai Waitress,

Playboy Reject,

Nightclub Booker,

Daily Show Correspondent,

Sex Columnist,

Recurring Character,

and Whatever Else

I, California

Stacey Grenrock Woods

SCRIBNER

New York   London   Toronto   Sydney

SCRIBNER
1230 Avenue of the Americas
New York, NY 10020

SCRIBNER and design are trademarks of Macmillan Library Reference USA, Inc.,
used under license by Simon & Schuster, the publisher of this work.

For information about special discounts for bulk purchases,
please contact Simon & Schuster Special Sales:
1-800-456-6798 or business@simonandschuster.com.

Text set in Bembo

Manufactured in the United States of America

1   3   5   7   9   10   8   6   4   2

Library of Congress Cataloging-in-Publication Data is available.

ISBN-13: 978-0-7432-7491-3
ISBN-10: 0-7432-7491-1

This work is a memoir. It reflects the author's present recollections
of her experiences over a period of years. Certain names and identifying
characteristics have been changed. Certain episodes are imaginative re-creations
and are not intended to portray actual events.

For Charlotte and Vi

CONTENTS

I, CALIFORNIA

HANUKKAH COMES ALIVE

Wading through a blue lake of presents in front of the living room fireplace, I felt bows, peeked in cards. Now it was quiet, but soon, sisters would arrive bearing gifts, they of fresh perms and flowing gauze robes. Sue would breeze in with her Siamese cat and her head full of big, mellow UC–Santa Barbara ideas. And Lee would heave bags and bags from the trunk of her BMW, all picked up on her rounds as a Hollywood wardrobe stylist. There'd be lots of chitchat about ferns, jogging, pool covers, maybe brewer's yeast, as we gathered in the gold and powder blue living room to open all the boxes that had been accumulating during this, the festival of lights. Soon, I'd surely have more socks, nightgowns, and maybe even a calculator. Oh, to be six years old and upper middle class. There was nothing like it.

My brother Cary (fifteen, fierce) doled out the presents while Lee gave each of us something called a "truffle." My sister styled Alpha Beta commercials, working closely with the supermarket chain's spokesman, a certain Mr. Alan Hamel. She'd regale us with stories of the malfunctioning Alpha Beta "Tell A Friend" promotional wagon, and of the antics of Hamel's girlfriend, a struggling actress named Suzanne Somers. "You know what she went and did?" Lee would say. "She put a divider between her clothes and his clothes so they wouldn't touch, can you believe that?" Suzanne sometimes went on Alpha Beta shoots as an unpaid makeup artist so she could sip from the cup of fame, even if it was just a Styrofoam cup of tepid craft service bouillon. She'd pull up to the set in her old donkey of a Mercedes and make jokes with the crew. These bitter, powdery balls, these truffles from Hollywood, so different from Hanukkah gelt my mom and I bought at the supermarket, or even the Hershey's Kiss assortments we'd gotten everyone as gifts from me, were favorites of the Hamel-Somerses.

For every one present for someone else, there were about three for me, the baby, and of course everyone got lots of presents from Corky. The evergreen forest of laughs we'd get from the image of our black cockapoo at the hardware store, paying for, say, a socket set, reached as far as the eye could see. How does she do it, do you think? How did she find the thing, and get it up to the counter? Does she have a wallet, or did she just carry the money in her teeth? It was funny to imagine!

But what was this? Among the to's and from's surfaced a peculiar gift—a white teddy bear wearing a red and green knit cap and a sweater with Christmas trees and the words

"Jingle Bear" on it. This was odd, since resisting the Christmas aesthetic was part of what we, the chosen crew, had to do to convince ourselves that our holiday was also good. "It was a free gift with purchase," my mother stammered. "They just gave it to me at the Broadway for spending twenty-five dollars. Can you believe that?" No, wow, we all laughed nervously, we could not believe it. Free gift with purchase. Huh. But what price was free?

The first gift was labeled "from Dad to Mom," but really, he explained, it was a gift for all of us: it was a frozen yogurt maker! Now we could make our favorite dessert at home. The people of Sherman Oaks, a progressive little settlement nuzzled on the graceful shoulder blade of Beverly Hills, were among the first to embrace this modern delicacy, this frozen yogurt. Other towns would have surely shunned it. Smaller minds might have cowered (*Yogurt?* With the satisfaction and mouth feel of ice cream? That's the devil's work!). But out here in Sherman Oaks, we couldn't believe it was yogurt before *you* couldn't believe it was yogurt.

Next was a gift to me from Lee—a hardbound copy of *The World's Greatest Fairy Tales*. Good, I liked fairy tales, and these were the world's greatest, so even better. A solid gift. One to cherish for years and years to come. What's next? I opened another present to even the numbers, choosing a tube-looking thing from my brother. It was a poster. Of my favorite singer. Peter Frampton. Playing the guitar. Look, everyone! It's Peter! I held up the top like the head of a poisonous snake, and the poster all at once unfurled itself, overtaking my body, finally writhing and settling in a shiny black coil in my lap.

As someone else took a turn, I came face-to-face with Peter, and discovered that he hadn't buttoned his shirt, and his sweat-moistened chest was completely exposed! This can't be! What was I going to do? Peter Frampton, with all his brazen maleness, was more than my fluttering soul could take. Below his toffee-colored foaming tendrils, the open satin shirt exposed a feathery spray of hair, like the wings of a rare Bengalese finch unfolded across his chest. My idols didn't have chest hair, and if they did, they at least had the decency to keep it to themselves. Ol' Pete Frampton, who was probably at this moment innocently eating beans on toast across the pond, had opened a Pandora's shirt of troubles for me. Okay, yes, I wanted him to show me the way, and baby, I loved his way, and I wanted to tell him I loved his way, wanted to be with him night and day, but that was between me and him. And Corky got everyone socks.

My Corky socks sat untouched. "Stacey, is everything okay? Do you like your poster?" asked Sue, all peasant skirts and hash. "Where are you gonna put your poster, Stacey?" asked my brother.

"Uh, in my room, I guess." My room, where Bambi lived, and everything was edged in yellow gingham, and there were toy ovens and paintings of little girls with real yarn for hair.

"She's embarrassed! Because his shirt is open!" cried Sue. "She's embarrassed. Awwww!"

No, I wasn't!

Yes, she is, she's embarrassed!

Great, this was exactly what happened after they took me to my second screening of *Tommy,* when I remarked

4

that I had enjoyed the performance of Roger Daltrey, also shirtless.

"My turn!" said my mother, shifting the attention. "And I'm opening this one from," she squinted at the tag, "Stacey!" This was a present Lee had helped me make. It was called a memory box, a popular craft of the seventies, fashioned out of a stained wooden box with lots of compartments and a glass top. You filled each section with a different dry good— barley, corkscrew pasta, white beans, hearthy things to connote warmth, nourishment, and general woman-ness, and then you hung it on the kitchen wall. Mom loved it. The women of Sherman Oaks revered craft. They were the original jewelry-in-the-garage-makers, ceramics-class-takers, the bread-dough-shellackers, never afraid to roll up their raw silk sleeves and put that glaze-it-yourself attitude to work.

In the top center box, we re-created a little scene from one of Lee's personal memory boxes: a little swirl of twigs to indicate a fake nest with a half an eggshell nestled in the center. It was something I'd stare at whenever I visited her apartment. I so wanted to touch it, to crouch in that tiny nest with that real egg.

My best friend, Ushio Terashima, and I had spent all of kindergarten building our own girl-sized nest in a remote corner of the playground. On the last day of school I climbed into the nest and rested on my stomach, wings folded, toes pointed out like a tail.

"Tweet, tweet," I chirped. "Tweet, tweet!"

Ushio ran over, her face buckled in anguish. "What are you doing?" she shouted. "You can't get in! You're messing up the nest!"

I bolted to my feet. "I thought," I whimpered, my hands trembling before my face, "I thought we were gonna be birds!" But I had thought wrong. In Ushio's mind, the nest should never be used, never trampled or upset. Never have eggs laid into it, or baby birds hatched within. Never should worms be vomited down little bird throats, nor should one watch those birds fly away from it. Ushio pounded her fists on the asphalt as I stood there, twig parts clinging to the front of my sunny yellow dress. Yes, the nest must stay chaste. How Japanese.

And here I had always tried to be so careful, especially whenever I visited the Terashimas' quiet, quiet house, where the loudest sound was the *scrape scrape scrape* the spoon made when her mother mixed Bundt cake icing in an aqua plastic bowl. I'd stay in the bathroom for what seemed like forever, trying to make the tear of the toilet paper just perfect, so no one would think I was some kind of dirty Jew.

"Okay, these little blue presents," announced Lee, "Dad and Cary need to open at the same time!" Dad and Cary regarded their new silver Tiffany key chains with casual bafflement. They knew, to some degree, that they had to put on a brave face and at least pretend to be impressed by this attempt to inject a little pizzazz into their pockets. It reminded me of the time we ate dinner at Lee's small apartment, and the girls ate off china at the table and my father and brother were served on iron plates on the couch. My sister, faced with having to delegate dishes judiciously, chose the iron plates for their masculine slant. The sight of my brother and dad banished to the other room and gnawing crudely on turkey legs made me so sad. The poor savages. Couldn't anyone help them?

Oh, look, a new basket for Lee! She really loved it. She said she planned to put it on the floor near her brown leather couch, next to her other baskets. There wasn't anything, we believed, that didn't look better in a basket, or with a basket nearby. Basket love was a privilege of the leisure class, really. You didn't need baskets, you didn't put them on your head and walk down to the river or anything. Baskets simply said, "Look at me, I am here, and that is that." This one had a handle, and came from Lee's favorite store, a place called the Pottery Barn, which was a totally new concept: barn chic. Hurricane lamps, wineglasses, and beeswax candles were displayed on bales of hay. Everything was white, clear, or hay-toned, the kind of minimalist shed where livestock might pass the night swirling white zinfandel around in thin-stemmed globes while chatting about Antonioni, eventually coming to the realization that everything their parents told them was wrong. Lee's apartment was that kind of place, where I loved to sit, gazing at photography books for hours beneath the creeping charlies and skylights.

Everyone was basically out of presents, but I still had a few more. There were bubbles (neat!), a calculator (at last!), and more socks from Corky, who just wanted everyone's feet to be warm. And there was a curious slim package from Sue. "Open it," she cooed. It was something I didn't recognize, a long black leather thing with a handle and a loop at the end. "It's a riding crop," she said, "for your saddle!" Everyone made the customary ah's of passive endorsement, but my brother groaned and rolled his eyes. "Come on, what's she gonna do with that?"

Two years earlier, my sister was styling an industrial film for Pennzoil that was to feature a little girl in the Old West buying penny candy from an old-fashioned candy store. There was an issue with the hair color of the girl who had been cast—it was too light, complained the director, "no one's gonna believe this shade of blond in a boomtown!" Because I was the sister of the stylist, and my hair was the right color, and I already had my own prairie girl dress, I was in. All I had to do was point to the candy in the case, and bloom my hand to expose the shiny penny in the center of my palm. The concept had something to do with the goodness of copper, and was meant to remind us how much we all loved and trusted copper. See? Look what a little copper can do. This darling child uses it to buy penny candy, for fuck's sake. All day long, I pointed and bloomed, pointed and bloomed. I could've done it forever. Could've done it for days on end.

And later, I was allowed to spend my $360 paycheck on whatever I wanted, so, of course, I bought a brand-new child-sized western saddle. I didn't have a horse, but I assumed if I had the saddle, the horse would just materialize and be patiently waiting for me in the garage. Until that day, the saddle would sit stiffly on a metal rack in the family room, where I would ride it, every night, in a nonsexual manner.

"Leave her alone," my mother said, gathering up wrapping paper. "She likes to ride her saddle." Everyone repaired to the dining room, while the Jingle Bear sat alone, unclaimed.

Days went by, and my poster stayed rolled up among the ruffled pillows of my window seat. One night, as hot dogs and buns steamed in our Coney Island Home Hot Dog Steamer, I bounced dutifully up and down on my saddle, whipping the rack with my riding crop, and thinking long and hard about Peter Frampton.

I recognized the delicate shame I was experiencing—it was as if he knew what was happening inside me, and thought it was funny. Like, when I used to look at David Cassidy in my View-Master—his glossy hair, his removed elegance—and was immediately and inexplicably overcome with dishonor. It was as if he knew that, as a baby, I wore diapers.

I hung the poster on the back of the door, and kept the door open.

I was not a prudish kid by any means. I'd seen *Cabaret,* I'd seen *Tommy* twice. I knew that the lyric in David Bowie's "Hang Onto Yourself" that went "we move like tigers on Vaseline" was a metaphor for the sex act. I liked to think I was as progressive as, or perhaps more progressive than, most first graders. It was just that, you let a few chest hairs slip by, and then, before you know it, you have to admit that everyone, including yourself, is real. You've grown up and you're not special anymore. No one carries you if you don't feel like walking, you'll be expected to have all your forms in order, you get the appropriate amount of presents, and you can be seated in an exit row on a plane. When you go out to eat, your menu doesn't turn into a hat, your menu stays a menu, with the same three pastas, four salads, four entrées, crème brûlée or flourless chocolate cake as everyone else's.

And after a while, your dreams die.

And after your dreams have been dead for a while, you join a warehouse club store and start buying in bulk. One day, you'll come home with a big box of Costco croissants, and the ones you don't eat, you freeze.

And then you'll defrost them, and eat them, one by one, and if you drop one, you'll pick it up. You won't worry about how you look when you bend down. "No one's looking at me," you'll tell yourself. And then, no one is. You brush off that defrosted warehouse club croissant with your fingers.

And eat it.

You grow old, you grow old, you grow old, you shall wear the bottoms of your relaxed-fit jeans rolled, and some Rockport walking shoes, and a visor.

A visor.

I still remember the first time I heard of death. I was playing with a roly-poly bug at the bottom of the daisy hill in the front yard, and my brother said, "If you keep rolling that bug up like that it's gonna die."

No, no, no, you're mistaken. Not this bug. This bug will never die. "Yes, it will," he said. "Everything dies. That bug will die, I'm gonna die, you're gonna die."

Me? Die? Everyone? Die? I searched my brain for the person I honored most in the whole world, the person who seemed the most invincible.

"Do you mean to tell me that one day, Carol Burnett is going to die?"

"Yeah, Carol Burnett, Harvey Korman."

"What about Vicki Lawrence?"

"Vicki Lawrence, all of *Mama's Family*. They're all gonna die."

And stay dead—not like Harold in *Harold and Maude*, which my sisters had taken me to see when I was younger.

But now, every moment was marked. Every holiday, every birthday: death, death, death. At the turn of the seventies, we acknowledged my mother's birthday. I remember my pretty, pretty mom, sitting alone at the table, looking frowsy and menopausal in her thin yellow housecoat. Before her was a birthday dessert, an unstructured pie of sorts, barely candled, whose sinister, calculated uncalculated-ness seemed to snicker, "The eighties are here, fuckers." This was the beginning of the end, I knew it then. There would be no more cakes, only shapeless birthday fruit slumps. Make a wish!

In the following years, red and green bows sprouted in the Hanukkah pile. Eventually, full-fledged Santa paper. My brother, the person who taught me what mortality was, grew a mustache, gathered up his jazz fusion records, and made off for San Diego State University, where he felt he could breathe, and learn accounting. Sue was gone, too. She had traded her Indian jewelry and macramé bathing suits for the stodgy, deep-dished marriage and family life of Chicago. The coast, with its roadside date stands and carob clusters, those stolen sips of Kahlúa on summer nights, all left behind. My parents' eyes were questioning, as if to say, "Why is she leaving? We gave her the sun. And volleyball."

No one got me any more horse accoutrements. That horse, it turns out, *was* the world's greatest fairy tale.

But my parents and I still took down the menorah and

lit it every year. Our menorah wasn't the typical kind, but a stone carving of a bunch of hopeful-looking Jews, whose upstretched palms formed the candle slots. I noticed for the first time the detail with which the sculptor had rendered their individual expressions. How whiny they looked. Like a big bunch of saps.

Lee married a photographer. I met him for the first time when they took me to see *Manhattan,* and on the way home, he held my shoe out the window the whole way while I screamed, "Give me back my shoe! I don't even know you!"

At the end of the movie, Woody Allen tries to convince young Mariel Hemingway not to go to London to study acting. He's worried she'll change, and he doesn't want her to. But it's too late, her bags are packed and her ticket has been bought. "Six months isn't such a long time," she tells him, "and besides, everyone gets corrupted." Or does she say, "*not* everyone gets corrupted"? I've played the DVD a million times and I've never been able to tell.

My brother and I saw Peter Frampton play at a tiny club south of Los Angeles in the nineties. Backstage, the ogres of security guided Peter through the various locks and high-level-clearance areas they created for him so that perhaps he'd never notice he wasn't stepping onto the stage at the Forum. As they maneuvered him into the wings, I saw a glimpse of his little head and thought, How his hair is growing thin.

I think about that Jingle Bear sometimes when I take my solitary, meditative morning walks. Did anyone take it home?

And on one of my solitary, meditative morning walks, it occurs to me that this is the coolest August L.A. has had since I can remember, but I still have to walk early, otherwise, it's just too hot. I wear comfortable shorts, and because I want to protect my face from the sun's harmful rays, I wear a visor.

A visor, yes. But no Rockports. Not now, not ever.

TELL STACEY

SHE'S A BAD WRITER

Not long ago, I was the victim of a very typical and boring offense: I was receiving a constant stream of unsolicited e-mails from a stranger, or group of strangers, with attachments that reeked of virus. I'd get about six a day, and each baited me with the kind of eerie, horrid sentiments that mostly come on the wings of nightmares: "It's you!" and "Why did you say that?" and "Is this your account?"

Now, I'm not some sixty-seven-year-old man with a vanilla-colored PC and new slip-on tennis shoes. I don't fall for such scams.

But one morning, the virus went too far. It said, in lowercase:

"you are a bad writer."

What on earth? How did this roving band of cyber-punks know I was a writer, and a bad one, no less?

It's not as if I don't try to be better, I do. And it's not as if I don't try hard, I do.

There are those who sit in metropolitan bars and say, "My dream is to have a place in the country where I can just write and write and write." That is not my dream. There are those movies that start with a couple moving to a little house in a little town where the husband finally has what he's always wanted: a writing room. I don't care for those movies.

Too often, as the rest of the city busies itself with suc-ceeding in offices of sea foam and bisque, lunching in restaurants where the water is icy and the pain rustica is powdery, their handheld devices aflame with deals, deals, deals, other people's deals, I might be on the back porch, sipping PG tips tea and looking at the perfect, violet morn-ing glories (the dear morning glories) twisting up the tele-phone pole, or the buff-colored faces of celebrities in magazines. (God, how I love to gaze at them.) It's okay, I think. Let them do what they will, let them sip their icy water, let them have their basil. I am a writer, and I am sleepy under the weight and heat of my complex, difficult, shimmering thoughts. Let me rest, I need to rest.

That's when the Listing Nag comes to me. She's an ethereal being, bent over a little at the waist, wearing a housecoat. Usually she has a Cockney accent and a nasty, Mrs. Andy Capp sort of disposition, perhaps a head rag. She's mean to me.

"And what about that book you 'ad to 'ave? That Marsle

Prowst book you said, 'Ooo, it's the best thing e'er written, it is, 'ave to 'ave it, I do! Need it for me inspiration, like. 'Aven't even touched it, 'ave you? Salman Rushdie works from ten-thirty to four every day."

He does not.

"'Ee does so, I read it in the *Observer*. And 'e 'as a fatwa, 'e does! Why can't you do that? Other writers do all kinds of things. They don't 'ave nice computers and DirecTV. They sit in little crap places and eat nofing and do whatever they 'ave to do. They don't 'ave Whole Foods round the corner! They don't even 'ave tuppence!"

She's so mean to me.

She doesn't understand how hard it is. I once had to write a paper in college on a Toni Morrison book. I sat on the floor of my little Sherman Oaks apartment with its powder blue carpet and white wicker loveseat where most people have proper couches. I put on the soundtrack to *The Hunger,* as always, and hovered around the paper, wincing, all day. I wrote longhand, I cried, I panted, I had some soup, I utilized the thesaurus, and I came away with four sentences, all about women's necks and hollowness, and being rootless. The inspiration for all this came from a phrase very early on in the book. It was the first sentence.

I received an A+ on the paper, which only reinforced my silly methodology. I am a seal. If you reward me, I'll keep doing it.

In sixth grade, I was, like all the other sixth graders, in love with short little Scott Silver. At the time, his diminutive stature and amiable bone structure were considered very attractive by all of us, but poor Scott didn't fare well.

Years later I ran into him between classes at community college. He was still short, and now he carried his shortness in a perverted way, his nose had become a greasy beak, and his limbs looked like thick flippers. He tried to laugh off something about a court order and liking speed too much, but we both had to get to our next class. Mine was creative writing, and I don't remember what his was.

But in sixth grade, Scott was a prince. Certainly, one could go out on a limb and be into Warren, but to do so would be to assert that one was immune to the draw of S. Silver, and that was unlikely. His hair swooped across his forehead as if spilling from a chocolate fountain in a penthouse in Manhattan on New Year's Eve. No, the top of the Chrysler Building on New Year's Eve. The caliber of chocolate fountain that can only be perforated by the marshmallows of kings.

I liked Scott, and the word around the school catering truck was that Scott was about to ask me to go with him. Just "go with." At our little adobe-style, midpriced private school, it was "go with," and sometimes just "go." I hadn't been this elated since the Ayatollah released the hostages!

I went home that afternoon and cleaned my room. Everything felt so good.

It was high time to reimagine the yellow gingham wallpaper-covered bulletin board that hung on my wall, untouched since fifth grade. I took down the picture of the monkey carrying skis and replaced it with a subtler photo of a keeshond I had ripped from a magazine. I considered taking down last year's report on Ambrose Bierce's "An Occurrence at Owl Creek Bridge," but left it up since I had gotten an A+ on it. I put up a "Ski Mammoth" button, took down the puka shells from Hawaii, moved the picture of me with a black eye in the park, centered the postcard from Spain of the dancing lady with castanets and a real fabric skirt, threw away my whale-watching certificate and "Quiet as a Mouse" Paper Plate Award (the brainchild of an overzealous nursery school teacher), and did some general straightening.

After TV, I drank a milkshake and went to bed, thinking everything was just fine.

Everything was not just fine.

I hadn't noticed that the little satellite hovering around called Michelle, or "Mikki," Cohen had been gaining in prominence in recent weeks. Mikki had always been on hand at all the South of Ventura Boulevard private school pool and spin-the-bottle parties. She wore the clothes, she walked the walk, she cheered the cheers, she was just one of those. Her blond hair draped across her forehead like a blond chocolate drape. It was otherwise short, like a boy's, like Scott's, in fact, but blond chocolate, and not from a fountain—from maybe a dime store. She was not competition; no one in her right mind would consider Mikki Cohen competition. She was an imitator, an afterthought, unnecessary, an atmospheric player. When, on a movie set, the second AD calls upon the extras to start moving before the "action" is called by yelling "background!" it's a sea of Mikkis he's talking to. She was a bouquet of routine white tulips at the very back of the bridal magazine, the overkill your eye cannot process because you've just taken in three-hundred-plus pages of first-rate florals by the best stylists in the business. The ones who don't follow trends, but create trends.

I would've at least understood had it been Jiffy Reiter. Jiffy Reiter was a credible threat. Those woeful, down-tipped eyes, probably settled that way through generations of surveying tables of fresh-baked streusel, her tan, even nostrils fluted like petals, taking it all in. Oh, I'll never forget the time my mother and I sat in our car and shared a canister of shoestring potatoes as we watched this so-called "prettiest girl in school" from the pickup parking lot.

"Her?" She coughed, wiping her fingers on some crumbling purse-pak tissues. "That one? Oh, gimme a break—she's no match for you."

Really, Mom?

"Look at her. Stiff arms. Fat forehead."

I guessed she was right, but I still thought Jiffy was prettier than I. Her mother's Volvo pulled up, and as Jiffy got in, a just-clipped putty-colored curl grazed the high collar of her shirt. She had worn it last week, too, the one with the small daisy pattern and the skinny burgundy ribbon around the neck. Last week she did it with brushed denim jeans, but today she wore it with the mauve cords, braided belt.

I think she owns a B-and-B in Sedona now. She never went with Scott. I think she was into Warren.

And I don't think I ever ate shoestring potatoes again.

On the day Scott was supposed to ask me to go with him, I showed up at school to learn that he had already asked Mikki. And she had accepted.

Mikki? Why Mikki?

What did Mikki have that Scott needed? He must've

liked girls who had the same name as a noted mobster—
something I found out one day when my dad heard I was
going to Mikki Cohen's house. He told me to watch out for
machine gun fire, which I didn't really get until about fifteen years later.

It was her birthday party, a typical affair seeped in Encino
ranch home pleasures: a giant sub, cut in pieces, girls in the
latest novelty socks, forced swimming. I noticed Mikki's
mother had the same swollen, thick eyelids and Muppet
nose (the long beak style, for the humanlike ones) as Mikki.
She also had one of those expensive KitchenAid mixers
with all the attachments.

I came home and told my mother about the mixer.

"Hmm," she said, and then nothing else. That $300
mixer had so many attachments, and I knew she was
thinking about the dough hook particularly. She thought
about dough hooks sometimes. It was okay.

What was to become of me while Scott and Mikki
played out their courtship against the backdrop of our tiny,
midpriced, adobe-style private school society? What would
I do while Scott was being welcomed into the Cohen
home, into the Cohen hearth, to sprawl in the light that
shone through their sparkling clean windows and bounced
off all those radiant copper gelatin molds?

My life and all its nuances would stay about the same, I
supposed. I'd still get shit for not finishing my lamb chops,
I'd write in my diary, attend other sub/swimming parties,
drink milkshakes at bedtime, and occasionally pretend to
be a DJ with my brother's stereo when he wasn't around.
(I'd put on the headphones, and swirl around in the swivel

chair, playing all my favorite songs and stealing glances of myself in the dresser mirror. "Hey, that was 'Double Life' by the Cars, and before that, we heard Yes with 'All Good People.' " It was very innocent, and I've long since forgiven myself for it.)

Running into my room, I grabbed my little red diary with the gold-dusted edges, opened it to a blank page, and carved, taut-fisted, "FUCK SCOTT, FUCK MIKKI. THEY'RE PROBABLY FUCKING ANYWAY," diagonally across the page. I then flung my diary into a corner and never wrote in it again.

I had done something to cause this. It was the only explanation: yesterday Scott liked me and today he did not. What had I done?

I had rearranged my bulletin board, that's what I'd done. I had taken down the monkey with skis and puka shells, replaced them with the keeshond picture and a "Ski Mammoth" button, and made a lot of other adjustments and, in doing so, I must've altered the energetic composition of the universe and Sherman Oaks. For whatever reason that I didn't need to understand, my thoughts on Ambrose Bierce's short story "An Occurrence at Owl Creek Bridge" were obviously positioned just so to touch off a chain reaction that went from the bulletin board, to the "Quiet as a Mouse" Paper Plate Award, to the black-and-white photo of me with a black eye in the park, across the bread-dough mermaid, over the yellow carpet, into the living room, past the pussy willows in the antique ceramic boot, out across the street, over the tops of pine trees, jacaranda trees, magnolia bushes, onto Ventura Boulevard, up a wooded path, and straight into Scott Silver's testicles. I learned the hard way, and too late.

None of my old things were still in my yellow gingham wallpaper–covered wastebasket. I checked the kitchen trash and there they were, the wrinkled remnants of my positive molecules, underneath the folded *Greensheet* paper and some empty packets of Gaines Burgers. Oh, Gaines Burgers. How I loved to crumble the moist meat-and-cheese-colored mush into the bowl like they did on the commercial. I'd often overfeed our dog just because I loved to crack the Gaines Burger and let its worms sift through my fingers.

But there would be plenty of time for that later, after I undid the careless damage of the day before.

Once everything was back in place, I carried on like nothing was wrong, all the while trying not to think about the small greasy stain on the Paper Plate Award, and the endless ways the trash could've contaminated it. I had reversed the damage. I had turned negative back into positive, odd back to even, two back to zero, bad back to good. I had. I had.

It was time to do my journal writing for the week. My journal was not the same as my diary, not at all. The journal was a teaching aid of our sixth-grade English teacher, the asshole Mrs. Puth, who had called our whole class snobs earlier in the month. If we wrote seven pages a week, we automatically got an A, six pages, a B, and so on down the line. It didn't matter what we wrote as long as it was of a certain length, so that we would develop a feel for the act of writing.

Valley School was up in arms when Mrs. Puth blew in

with her page requirements, her vaguely Asian features, and her shapeless cotton shifts. And her prejudice against us.

"What? She doesn't even read them?" said the Encino-based mothers.

"What kind of grading system is that?" they cried in Tarzana.

"I want my kid to be graded on his mer—"

No, Mom, we'd all say. We can write anything we want, it doesn't matter. It's the Year One now. We could write, "I had a very

very very very very very very very very nice summer," just to meet a space requirement if we wanted to, and some of us did, and some of us still do.

But I had been hard at work for some time on a serialized telling of a young person's story called "Robin," which was always written with a little flower next to it. Robin❀ was about a girl, a girl not unlike myself, who had friends and a life very much like mine. Robin❀ had a friend named Marcy, who had no insignia because it wasn't her story, and the two of them did things. One time they went to a slumber party where they stayed up till five and made brownies with peanut butter and paprika in them! Just like I had recently done! And Robin❀ and Marcy often talked to each other and sometimes other girls from their class on the phone before and sometimes after dinner. (I did that, too.) They made plans. They were always about to do something, those girls.

Tonight, I settled into my pink heart-shaped satin pillow, dashed off a quick poem about how good grilled cheese is, an open-ended meditation on the breadth and slant of my handwriting, and began installment six.

Robin❀

Robin was home on Friday night, just waiting for Cheap Trick to come on the *Pink Lady and Jeff Show,* when the telephone rang. Robin slurped up the last of her milkshake and answered it.

"Hello?" said Robin.

"Hi, Robin," said the voice on the other line. It sounded like Marcy.

"Hi, Marcy," said Robin.

"This isn't Marcy," the voice said.

"What?" said Robin. "It isn't Marcy? Who is it?" asked Robin.

"Just kidding," said Marcy, "it's Marcy."

"I knew it was you," Robin said.

"No, you didn't," said Marcy.

"Well, who else could it be?" exclaimed Robin. "I know it's not Jacqueline because her family is in Lake Arrowhead this weekend, and I know it's not Shelly because, no offense, Marcy, you don't exactly sound like Shelly."

"Yah, I guess," said Marcy.

"How are you?" inquired Robin.

"I'm fine," replied Marcy.

"That's good," Robin said.

Just then, Robin's mom walked into the room and started ironing.

"Do you want to sleep over tomorrow night?" asked Marcy.

"Well," said Robin, "I'll have to ask my mom. Hold on."

"Okay," Marcy said.

Robin put the phone down and asked her mom.

"Mom, can I sleep over at Marcy's tomorrow night?"

"Well," said Mrs. Shell, "is it okay with Marcy's mom?"

"My mom," said Robin to Marcy, "wants to know if it's okay with your mom."

"Yah, I already asked her," exclaimed Marcy.

"Yah, Mom," explained Robin, "it's okay with Marcy's mom. She asked her already."

Mrs. Shell thought for a moment. "Well, okay." She smiled.

Robin went back to the phone. "Yep, my mom says it's okay."

"Okay, come over at seven."

"Okay, 'bye."

"'Bye."

What would Robin❀ and Marcy do the next night at the sleepover? And what would Robin❀ do until then? I sat and wondered. They could make cookies at the slumber party, I guessed, but I had already explored that territory and I kind of wanted to break them out of their safe places, which I could never do with Jody, the real-life Marcy.

Jody Jacobs was a fucking bummer. She was forever tugging on her plugged nose, which looked like a tiny spade shoveling cinnamon freckles and fear all over the rest of her face. She was generally afraid of doing fun things. Oh sure, occasionally she'd oblige and we'd drench her mom's tampons in water one by one, but so often she'd just sit there and mope. She rarely wanted to call the party line, and one time, when I very nicely tried to teach her some piano chords, she couldn't even get her fingers to make a C. I showed her how easy it was, one finger at a time, but she got to the point where she couldn't put a single finger on a single key without crying.

"Are you kidding me? Are you telling me you can't put one finger on a key and press down?" (Sob, sob, sob. Sob, sob, sob.) "This is unbelievable! What's the matter with you?"

I sent her home with a nice, detailed diagram I had drawn (my dad is an artist, so I can draw really well) of the parts of a tap shoe and told her to be familiar with it the next time we got together.

Marcy was kind of like Jody in the sense that she had glasses, but Marcy was less of a baby.

Even so, I thought maybe the reader had grown accustomed to Robin and Marcy's movements as I had established them so far, and might respond to a Robin and Marcy who went beyond preconceived expectations. But who was I kidding? There wasn't any reader.

Impassioned writing had felt good when I had done it earlier that day ("FUCK SCOTT, FUCK MIKKI. THEY'RE PROBABLY FUCKING ANYWAY") and, as long as no one was reading, there was something else I needed to say.

Midway through page six, I wrote a title in all caps: WE ARE NOT SNOBS.

I drew a flower next to "SNOBS" and continued.

We are not snobs. I don't think it's right for you to call us that. You don't even know us. If someone's book bag is falling apart, I personally don't see what's wrong with telling them so they can get a new one. That doesn't make someone a snob. I know the person who said it and she's not a snob at all. She's really nice. I think you are just prejudiced against us because we are a gifted class, but just because we are gifted, it doesn't make us bad. Also, your class doesn't challenge me. Last year, in Mrs. Biederman's class, we learned a lot more. Ask anyone. She believed in us and pushed us to do our best. That woman was more teacher than you'll ever be. She would never call us names.

Well, I've done my seven pages this week so sayonara! (That's Japanese for "good-bye," and "hello," and "peace.")

I still had some stuff to add to the unit I was working on about Jody, but there was no point in going on to page eight.

That night, I dreamed of Biederman, her hair—choco-brown drapes drawn back to expose a symmetrical face to rival Pam Dawber's—her handwriting, rounder than the roundest round: loops and circles as full and silky as oil in those ancient clay jugs the Egyptians used. "Excellent work, Stacey!" she'd write. "A+." My sister saw my *Uncle Tom's Cabin* book report on my bulletin board once and laughed. "Oh God," she snorted. "Look at that handwriting."

I saw what she meant, but I didn't agree. Mrs. Biederman was, after all, the woman who had given us all our first pens. There they were, a day before my birthday: black-and-white-striped Bics, waiting patiently on each desk as we filed in. I still remember their long stems, like plastic ink roses, and their fine, fine points. About half the kids, me included, took their new pens up to Mrs. Biederman's desk.

"Mrs. Biederman, I think you left your pen on my desk," we all deferred.

"No, guys." She grinned. "Those pens are for you."

Up until that point, no one had ever instilled in us the confidence of ink. Pencil was the way, always. But that was the thing about Mrs. Biederman, she believed more in us than we could ever imagine ourselves. She was Mindy to our just-hatched Morks. And she even wore the same barrettes as we girls did. How 'bout that?

Mrs. Puth, on the other hand, looked like she sewed her own clothes from dirty black sack cloth, and made soup from the dandelions she grew on the side of her garage.

The next day at school was uneventful. I turned in my journal, stared at the spiky, sweat-infused hairs above Charlie Graver's neck. I had been looking at them for two years. We sat in alphabetical order.

The phone call came as I was enjoying my nightly milk-shake in front of the TV. Thin traces of Phisoderm still resonating from my cheeks, I raised the phone to my ear, said hello, and a voice said, "Tell Stacey she's a bitch."

And nothing more. I didn't recognize the voice, but I knew it belonged to a girl, roughly eleven, Caucasian, like every girl I knew. I just sat there dumbly for a while, as people do.

A bitch. Was I really a bitch? What had I done or said— that anyone knew about? I had done something, obviously.

I had conjured an accuser in the ether, an entity that loathed me. Was I really so bad? I loved grilled cheese, and my dog, and I pretended to like Yes so that my brother might think I was cool. But I've never really liked Yes. And I don't think he ever did think I was cool. I guess he wasn't alone. I may have been an acquired taste in my copper-colored satin jeans and hair that rippled and sank like the caramel in a candy commercial, but I meant no harm. I walked the walk, I cheered the cheers, I laughed at Carla the dumb girl. I fit in fine.

Was it someone related to those mean boys who spit on my head on the whale-watching boat that time?

Was it Wendy Kendall from my old school, whom I kicked in the stomach when she twisted the rings so that I would twirl around uncontrollably on the ring thing? I don't know about anybody else, but I think you're well within your rights to put your foot out when someone has caused you to twirl around uncontrollably on the rings, and if you just so happen to kick the person who did it, so be it. I don't want to live in a world where you can't put your foot out and possibly kick the person who twisted the rings in order to cause you to twirl around uncontrollably.

I had the entire weekend to think about who it could've been.

On Saturdays, a few of my friends and I attended a class put on at Bullock's department store and cosponsored by *Seventeen* magazine. It was sort of an all-around grooming, style, modeling, health-and-beauty deal taught by a former model named Nelda Short. Nelda, besides having the most beautiful name a girl could ever want, lived with her husband in Manhattan Beach, put her makeup on in the kitchen where the light was good, and had had so many botched nose jobs that she huffed like a Pekingese. She couldn't really laugh the catty laugh we all sensed she wanted to laugh, but when she'd disapprove of, say, someone's hair or outfit, she'd do a pinchy little nasal snort and say, "Huh! Not *too* attractive." My public school friend, Linda, and I said that well into junior high.

The lure of the class was that Nelda seemed to have some nebulous connection to *Seventeen* magazine, and if you were hot enough, she could maybe possibly be your in. I don't think anyone ever claimed that, it was just assumed by us preteens and our moms, who figured that, either way, we'd "get something good out of it." We were taught things like "if you don't go number two every day, something's wrong, guys" and how to put together your modeling portfolio. She showed us hers—glossies of her legs reveling in the sheerness and comfort of a certain panty hose, on a shiny black stage wearing a *Chorus Line*–type getup, and walking through the park, just daydreamin'. I've always remembered the last photo in the book, which was of Nelda throwing her sailor-hatted head back with a big, openmouthed smile and a wink. We all loved it. "Always leave 'em with a winner," she said.

That Saturday, we were learning about makeup. We learned about makeup a lot. I didn't think any of the girls in the class could've been the one who called me. Most of them didn't have my phone number, and the ones who did loved me.

Nelda had brought in some of her personal cosmetics to show us how models use them. Snore! I already knew how models used them. I'd had the fucking Christie Brinkley book for like a year.

"The important thing to know about mascara is, you should never use anyone else's mascara," said Nelda.

Suddenly, Jody perked up and trumpeted forth like a Dickensian Christmas morning: "And you should always wipe off the blob at the end onto a Kleenex!" She then gave a quick, almost invisible tug to her nose and melted backward, so satisfied. "My cousin's a nurse," she explained.

No one said much. We were all of us quite stunned, Nelda included. Jody was always looking for the perfect time to trot out "my cousin is a nurse." She held on to it like a piece of cashmere worn thin from constant stroking. The girl had such weird timing. She made me nuts. If only she knew no one gave a crap.

It was time to rethink what it was that originally drew me to Jody.

Mrs. Puth hadn't given our graded journals back yet, but I had some stuff I wanted to add to the unit on Jody, like how she would call someone "the blob of the century," as if she were so skinny herself.

But really, who could've called me? I hoped it wasn't someone from my class, not after the way I stood up for everyone in my journal. Could it have been Debbie Moscow, from back in public school? She was a little twat, to be sure, but would she do something like this?

I did make fun of her favorite song, something that went over badly in the Moscow residence, an altogether revolting place where the scent of hash zucchini bread wafted around the batik kitchen curtains, bobbed and weaved through the fronds of folk-art wall hangings, and nestled in the boggy brown carpet for later.

From its first little shoots, the Moscows had nurtured little Debbie's love of Manilow into a grand spreading oak. That love crested in a meltdown during the course of one birthday sleepover when Debbie simply would not stop playing "Mandy." The entire evening, "Mandy"; first thing in the morning during pancakes, "Mandy." It was her birthday and she wanted to hear it.

These were people who believed in letting their child express herself even if it meant this. Expression was revered in all its forms, even soft rock. Debbie's mom, whose body looked like a collection of potato dill loaves that ebbed and flowed below her purple gauze cloak, had almost surely cast her engorged breasts or sculpted her vulva at some point in her marriage, and presented it as a love token to Debbie's dad, a slouching, bearded figure with square glasses and an effeminate belt, who would have been profoundly touched by the gesture. On the weekends, they all went somewhere to hit each other with foam bats, I was sure of it.

I couldn't wait to be picked up from this hell. Rolling up my sleeping bag, I joked, "Hey, I thought he sent her away, why is Mandy back? She must be really stupid!" I thought for sure everyone else was with me on this, but they all just averted their eyes. In my house, the "Mandy" joke would have just been a given—making fun of someone like Barry Manilow was expected of you. Shit, in my house, you'd get your ass kicked for not heckling Manilow. You'd get lit cigarettes flicked at your eyelids while you slept, and a knee to the chest after that. You'd have to clean the rain gutters with nothing but a plastic spork from Kentucky Fried Chicken, and when you finished, you'd have to eat dinner with that same spork—a dinner of wet leaves from the rain gutters.

But here at Debbie's, I think people were a bit hurt.

I guess that's the thing that I've always failed to grasp: that some people really do like "Mandy." Some people like "Mandy" and some people are into Warren.

But could Debbie still be holding on to that? It was

years ago, before busing, and I never saw anyone (besides Linda) from public school anymore. Could it be that Debbie was now hanging out with the new inner-city friends she'd perhaps fallen in with, and they were all somewhere listening to *Off the Wall* and developing a hatred for me based on her recollections? Who was it? Who was out there, spreading lies about me? Thinking thoughts about me? Would I ever know, and would I ever be able to arrange and rearrange enough things to make it right, to set it back, to undo it? Nelda was, during this time, talking about cream blush, and I processed the lecture as "cream blush makes me feel bad, it makes me think bad things, must think about cream blush again to reverse damage." And I did, and I felt better. I fixed it. I controlled it.

I take pills for this now.

Monday afternoon. Charlie's sweaty, after-lunch hair stuck out from his neck like cleats. Mrs. Puth, dressed in one of her tough wraparound dresses, was handing back the graded journals, not saying much. She did not hand one to me.

She told everyone to silently study the week's spelling words, and called me up to her desk.

"Stacey, do you think this is an appropriate journal entry?" My journal sat on her desk, open to the page with WE ARE NOT SNOBS✸.

I didn't know. She told me that, well, she didn't think it was. There was another question, again about appropriateness, but this one applied to the manner in which you should address teachers. I didn't think I had addressed her wrongly, and I said something to that effect, but I was corrected. I was made to admit that I had been wrong to write what I had written, to defend myself and my peers against an accusation I felt was unjust, to have an opinion that differed from hers.

She told me she'd be keeping my journal entry in her permanent file, and without turning, she deposited a piece of paper into a file in a drawer to her right, and told me to go back to my seat.

It wasn't until years later, until today, actually, that I realized that she had just put some bullshit piece of paper into her drawer and had basically concocted this whole grave act just to scare me. I hadn't done anything wrong, she just didn't want to be criticized by an eleven-year-old in expensive jeans. No one does.

I'll bet she went home that night and had a great laugh over it. I'll bet that weekend, she got together with the few friends she still kept in touch with from the Peace Corps and they laughed and laughed about "the permanent file" until rice gruel went dribbling down their chins. I'll bet she thought it was as funny as the time she started a lesson by writing "Iran" on the board and saying, "Everyone's talking about Iran. Iran, Iran, and then I got tired." But I remember something, Puth. I remember that no one, not a single person, laughed at that. We all hated you.

Because you were a terrible teacher and you made us feel bad. It didn't matter that you were probably right. We probably were rotten little jerks, but telling us only made us worse. No one is helped by picking up the phone and hearing that she is a bitch. No one gets to be a better writer by getting an e-mail telling her she is a bad writer, even if it is just an anonymous virus. Life becomes little more than an anonymous virus, and what a person might do, especially if genetically predisposed to, is look around at everything she's touched and wonder what she did wrong to cause her to be infected by it. Did I place that plant wrongly? Did I cause people to dislike me because I put my sheets on upside down? Which one of these things did I do wrong? If someone could only tell me, then I can fix it. I swear I can fix it. I can cut and paste it, rewrite it, put it back the way it was. I can make it right with my mind.

That evening, I wrote the final installment of Robin❀.

On Sunday night, Robin was drinking a milkshake and watching *America's Funniest TV Bloopers* with her mom. They had spent most of the day at the mall, buying Robin a cute nautical top to go with her Guess? jeans. Robin was the first one at school to have a pair of Guess? and Marcy was jealous of her.

Just then, the phone rang. Mrs. Shell, Robin's mom, answered.

"Shell residence," she answered.

"Oh, yes. Hold on one moment, please."

Mrs. Shell put down the phone and said to Robin, "It's for you."

"Who is it?" asked Robin.

"Well," exclaimed her mother, "I don't know." She picked up the phone again.

"Can I ask who's calling, please? Well, okay then." She put down the phone. "They said it's your friend."

Robin rolled her eyes. Her mom was really great, but

sometimes she was annoying. Robin took the phone receiver.

"Hello?" Robin said.

"Hello?" repeated Robin. There didn't seem to be anyone there.

She said hello again.

"Hello?" and then a girl's voice she didn't recognize said, "Hello, is this Robin?"

"Yes," replied Robin, "this is Robin."

"Robin," started the girl, "um, you don't know me, but me and my friends just wanted to tell you—"

There was a long silence. Robin thought she heard other girls in the background.

"Um, we just wanted to tell you that we all think you're really great."

And the girl hung up before Robin could even say "thank you."

Robin put down the phone receiver.

"Who was that, dear?" asked her mother.

"Oh," said Robin, "it was just a friend."

Robin slurped up the rest of her milkshake and she and her mom laughed at the blooper of a news reporter getting butted by a goat. "This guy is really the butt of the joke!" laughed Robin. Her mother laughed also.

The End.

You always want to leave them with a winner.

Robin❀ was done, but from now on, I'd draw the flower next to my own name because it was my story, and I could write it any way I pleased. I could let my fingers linger in the soft, soft Gaines Burgers as long as I wanted.

It's just now occurring to me that it might have been Jody.

A MILE IN MY JAZZ SHOES

For me it came in mildly: in Sherman Oaks, in the amber hours after dinner when the family lolled around the TV and took to their pacific doings: needle-work, telephoning, watching *Ironside,* dreaming.

I wanted only to entertain.

"Everybody! Watch me, okay? Okay?" My mother would concede first, as mothers are wont to do. She'd make everyone stop doing what they wanted to do and watch me perform.

"This is a show about a lamb and her friends," I'd say, and launch into a little impromptu piece about a lamb, her friends, and their experiences in the meadow; there'd be a freestyle narrative and one or two songs, with dancing throughout. I played a dual role as the lamb and everyone else. Everyone always thought it was over so many times before it was over, and I'd have to constantly remind them

41

that I was still performing. That's called "breaking the fourth wall."

In later years (kindergarten, first grade), I tried always to expose my friends to the performing arts. I had been messing around with some choreography to "Big Spender" that I thought was pretty decent so I taught it to my friend Yuko. She wasn't bad, but her singing was a little flat in places and I had to do all of the advanced jumps. Linda was a great student, though, and we spent many afternoons carving out a massive routine to "Take Off with Us" from the *All That Jazz* soundtrack. When we were done, we dressed like stewardesses and debuted it for my mom, passing trays of hot mini-eggrolls as we danced. Had either of us seen the movie, maybe we would have realized that "take off" meant clothes, not airplanes, and that the whole number was an allegory for an orgy. Kids.

I'm still not sure at which point that little lamb of yesteryear, so innocent and eager for just a handful of sweet clover for her praise, turned into a stubborn, simpleminded ewe: I *must* entertain. They *will* watch me. I *am going* to make them know me. I will *stand here* until they hire me.

Years went by and one by one, my friends left Hollywood to be in other places, do other things. A speech therapist? Why? City planning? What in God's name for? Medical research in Riverside? Linda, you've got to be kidding me.

How will they know the world sees them? How will they know if they're loved, and how much? How do any of those people expect to know their worth? The world has to know you, otherwise, what's the point?

And once one commits to a life of show business, time is measured not in seconds, minutes, or hours, but by the consistent pulsing of your miserable, hot toes from inside Capezio jazz shoes (black ones or white ones or both); adolescent afternoons are spent not smoking Shermans and fitting in, but in dusty studios with eleven other girls in matching sweatshirts, rehearsing a modern jazz routine set to the *Magnum, P.I.* theme song.

Sometimes, if you forget you want to do it, it's only because you don't want to know if you want to do it. All you want to do is it, and you don't want to know what it's like not to want to want it anymore.

I've never known what's it like not to want to be famous.

And then at some point, everything just goes all wrong. You don't have the right look, you're not projecting your personality, you do not "pop." No one can picture you walking onto a sitcom set and saying "Hey!" really loudly. Other girls come, and they pop (oh, do they pop), and you stare at your audition makeup in your rearview mirror, not knowing what the hell to think anymore, and somewhere a strange man is touching your knee, your lamb is lost and so are her friends, the meadow is not where you left it, the old hug of the copper and black family room has gone all creamy and sterile and you're sitting in a waiting room with seven other girls who are also reading for the part of "Maggie, Eric's Girlfriend" and you see they all have on the same cute boot-cut jeans and sexy top. And you look down and see you, too, are wearing these jeans, this top, but you've never been more alone. When you stand up to go in

43

and read, you leave some spare blood on the floor around your chair, where it blooms, uncontained, like an oil spill. And yet you keep giving. You still offer your neck to the chopping block and say, "This is my neck, Madam Casting Director, please chop it." You give everything. No one knows giving like the performer knows giving.

I gave and gave and gave!

There is an underpopulated area just west of the treacherous Cahuenga Pass, which connects Hollywood and the San Fernando Valley (and where so many actors have lost their lives). Here, noble Ventura Boulevard, the pride of the Valley, mixes with the runoff of Hollywood. If you're coming from Sherman Oaks, you'll see the topography get sparser with every block, cute knickknack shops start to give way to naughty, drop-ceilinged motels with closed-circuit color televisions. There used to be bars called Residuals and The Casting Couch. It's no place for a child.

It's a mildly glamorous cove for the workhorses of the entertainment industry: the character actors, featured extras, recurring guest stars, soap actors, commercial actors, voiceover artists, people who always have a lab coat on them in case of a doctor audition, people who bring their own makeup to jobs, people whose résumés are thick with *Father Murphy*s, *Simon & Simon*s, and *Archie Bunker's Place*s, but whom you probably couldn't name or even classify as an actor. They belong to the special caste of human being who look familiar and America thinks it may have gone to high school with.

On this little strip of boulevard, between the giving way

and the running off, stands a building, flaky and dingy white. It's holding its head up high and giving its sagging neck some backhanded slaps in anticipation of its close-up.

Painted high on the wall in classic black script are the words "The American National Academy of Performing Arts Est. 1957." It's so stark that you might think to yourself, "Hmm, this must be a very official place indeed. The inclusion of both 'American' and 'National' is very intimidating. Am I an American National? May I attend?" and you go home and memorize the Preamble to the Constitution, just to be on the safe side.

I thought the name spurious even as a twelve-year-old. I knew no one in Washington had deemed this the official academy where the nation of America could learn scene study, musical comedy, ballet, tap, and modern jazz.

I'd be the youngest one there, in with girls up to age eighteen. My mom was a little concerned about the age gap, but I told her I didn't think I'd feel awkward about being so much younger, and, if anything, the eighteen-year-olds should be the ones who felt bad. I was ambitious. It was the eighties.

It wasn't the first performing arts school I attended, just the biggest. I'd been kicking around the drama, jazz, tap, ballet circuit in some form or another since I turned four. I'd taken private lessons, public lessons, summer sessions, park lessons, serious pink-tights-black-leotards-hair-in-a-bun-no-talking ballet lessons, stomp-on-the-floor-as-loud-as-you-want lessons, pretend-you're-bacon-frying-in-a-pan acting workshops, stare-into-your-partner's-eyes-and-convey-one-emotion-for-an-hour groups. I never stayed in any one place too long. A theatrical fluxist, I was. Perpetually in motion.

I'm recalling now an emblematic acting class taught by an emblematic, middle-aged woman who wore a clover green pantsuit and a bow in her unnaturally red hair. (The fringes of Hollywood are lousy with middle-aged women with bows in their hair.) We were having a postscene discussion.

"Now, students," she said, "how did you feel, what was your *emotion,* when Reggie's character came onstage and revealed his big secret?" The class was silent. "Stacey? How did it make you feel? What was your reaction when Reggie's character came onstage and revealed his big secret?"

I said that I had been astonished.

"Astonished!" she hooted, fingertips to chest. "Astonished! Well, well, well. That is quite a word for a young girl. Astonished! My goodness!"

Yes, it was quite a word. It was a neat word I had learned recently and now had occasion to use. So what?

"Astonished! My, my, what a sophisticated word! Did you hear that, kids? Stacey was *astonished.*"

I liked the word because tonally, it was similar to the name Anastasia—the long form of "Stacey" that my parents had not the romantic flair to name me but I'd pretend, sometimes, was my real name. Anastasia, astonish. Anastonisia. So pretty to my ears. So royal, so silky. The sounds looked like delectable, airy pastries injected with sweet cream and eaten with a warm drink cupped in the other hand while sitting, dreaming, in a little café whose tiny white octagonal floor tiles crept up the sides of the walls in Vienna.

When my mother came to pick me up, she, too, got word that I had been earlier astonished. I could tell Mom was subtly insulted that this woman (forty years too old for a bow) would think that her daughter wouldn't know a cosmopolitan word like "astonished." Of course she would! Her daughter knew all kinds of words. But this teacher just couldn't get her rusty head around it. Reflecting now, I wish I had known the word "cunt," because I would've used it then.

Maybe this new place would be better.

It wasn't, but after school on Tuesdays and Fridays (as well as all day on Saturdays) I'd race home from school, pull on one of my many unitard/sweatshirt/leg warmers/jazz shoes getups, pack my dance bag with all that I'd need, and Mom and I would drive down the four-mile Trail of Trepidation to the Academy. A long night of drama and dance lay before me, the dread of which filled my mouth with the sour memory of vomit—as if there were nothing more to vomit and hadn't been anything to vomit all winter. My stomach was a mix of metals unknown.

Inside the building was a quiet foyer, off which went some hallways and a string of irregular rooms (library? lounge? office? other lounge? other library?), each with gold-toned marshy carpets and the smell of soft dust. Plastic flowers and books and things soured in corners, where the little mushrooms grew and paint curdled, and now and then big wall plaques with hand-painted quotes reminded one:

"Our job, is to hold as t'were the mirror up to nature."
—Shakespeare

"Speak the speech I pray you, as I've pronounced it to you, trippingly on the tongue."—Shakespeare

"It's not what I say, it's how I say it. It's not what I do, it's how I do it."—Mae West

On one foyer wall were the framed headshots of all the favored students. "Stars of the Academy," it said above.

Let's see: there was Cathy, blond and braided and eighteen, the maidenhead of the Academy, apple-cheeked and Aryan flushed. She was the favorite, the bossy one, and also the tap teacher. She had a fresh smile, a big voice, big legs, and a small heart. She'd go on to be an extra in *The Best Little Whorehouse in Texas*.

And there was stout, Mediterranean Nancy, whom we rarely saw. You could imagine Nancy in lots of roles that had her laboring in a rustic kitchen, surrounded by hungry men, before whom she set down great bowls of fagioli and then stood back to curse at everyone in Italian with the tops of her wrists resting on her aproned waist. "I might get hit" was the vibe one got from Nancy. When we did glimpse her, it was usually just long enough to see her perform her signature song, the "Black Widow," before she vanished, in a flurry of applause, our own little pudgy Liza Minnelli. It was she who choreographed the *Magnum, P.I.* dance. I couldn't talk in her presence. In her headshot, she posed with a white bunny. Why?

Then there was D'arcy, a former student so limber that

she was actually known for her limberness. Her limberness was industry-famous. Think how limber you'd have to be in order for other dancers to notice. More than that. More so. More. Right about there. She took off her shirt in horror films.

And let me not forget the Czechs, Ingrid the older, and Karin the younger, two lovely sisters with enviable noses and brown round eyes like forest animals, but whose combined credits to this day add up to just one appearance as "Teenager 2" on *Trapper John, M.D.*

Notably missing from the star wall was the place's only connection to legitimate fame, former student Helen Hunt. Yes, Helen *Mad About You* Hunt. Academy Award–winner Miss Helen Hunt. Helen "Hells Bells" Hunt. Lady Helen Huntington of Huntsville. Helene de Tocqueville. Hell of the D'Urbervilles. The very same.

She was only ever alluded to and then only in whispers, vibrations, pulsations, thought pictures: "Helen Hunt went here." A cold current grazing your cheek seemed to say: "Helen Hunt went here." On stormy nights, the creaking of the old tree branch: "Helen Hunt went here." No one I knew had ever actually seen her. She wasn't even famous yet, she had only starred in a movie of the week about a high school girl who overcame obstacles to play on the boys' varsity football team, but it was more professional acting than all of us combined had done.

But she wasn't one of our stars. To be a Star of the Academy meant to be initiated into a special club that meant absolutely nothing to anyone for years and years to come. You were part of a long tradition of having your picture up on the wall. I was a fringe star because I didn't yet have a headshot to put on the wall, and a star without a headshot is no star at all.

The main room had a gold-carpeted riser for a stage and a heavy ceiling-to-floor curtain along the wall behind it. There was a little set: brocade loveseat, white rattan coffee table, dinette set, plate of Cheese Nips (hopefully), and a built-in shelf with just the essential props: plastic mugs, magazines, nylon flowers, wicker tissue box covers, and Spanish dancer figurines. The class sat in stackable chairs in what doubled as the main dance room.

The first human you'd likely encounter upon entering was Academy administrator Dorothy Barrett. She was an aged chorus girl and gingham enthusiast, as well as a relentless wearer of bows, who lived behind the locked door that led to the second floor of the Academy Where No One Ever Went. Her bright little half-moon eyes were in perpetual frenzied motion. Questions darted and dinged around like pinballs in her mind: "Who's doing, saying what, when? For how much? Why? All over the dance floor? About me? Who says? Since when?" When she listened to you, it was as if she were preparing to be slapped, but also as if she would like it just a little bit. Her cheeks were freckled and powdered, her mouth a slick of strawberry lipstick. A square mat of salt-and-pepper pin curls on top and old-lady-musical-comedy shoes down below rounded out the whole thing.

Dorothy let it be known at every turn that she had once shared a years-long, deep, abiding friendship with dearly departed screen legend and massive jerk Joan Crawford. If one were perhaps stepping into the office to deliver one's forty-dollar tuition payment for the month of April, one might be received with "Oh, thank you, dear. Will you just set it on the desk next to that photo of me and Joan Crawford? No, not that one, the other one. Oh, how I miss that great lady."

I was already familiar with Joan Crawford. Early on, my mother had instilled in me the bittersweet habit of going to the local branch of the public library and checking out books on subjects that interested me: psychology, makeup, teen modeling, psychiatry, horses, New York, the criminally insane, budgies. The very thought of it makes me weep fondly for the little person I was, standing at the card catalog, tiny pencil, tiny paper, sweet and new to everything.

At one point I got into biographies. I started with *Wired*, the John Belushi story by Bob Woodward. I read books about Marilyn Monroe and Elvis that held my interest for about ten minutes. Puzzlingly, I picked out a book by Roger Vadim that was sort of a love letter to his three ex-lovers (Catherine Deneuve, Brigitte Bardot, and Jane Fonda) called *Look at All the Exquisite Tail I've Gotten*, I think. But then I checked out a book called *My Way of Life*, written by, or I should say "dictated" by, Mommie Dearest herself. From the Acknowledgments: "I would like to thank Audrey Davenport Inman who for several months kept hitting me over the head to make me sit down at my tape recorder and finish dictating this book. It's not easy to produce a book when you're doing two other fulltime jobs, but Audrey made me do it."

Isn't that just about the nicest thing one professional can

say to another? Joan is grateful not because she considers the woman to be a competent editor, but because she believes the woman's true talent was getting her (Joan) to find the time to talk about herself into a tape recorder. And as for those two full-time jobs, I could only conclude that one was traveling around with her entourage and spreading the good news about Pepsi to (honestly) the jungles of Africa, and the other must've been "being nuts" because in 1973, when the book was published, when the only things holding her face to her skull were those two poised cobras she used for eyebrows, it certainly wasn't acting.

The cover is a picture of Joan, aged ninety or so, posed in front of a painting of who? Joan, silly! It looks to be painted by the caliber of artist whose specialty is those soft-hued, open-robed ladies that certain kinds of parents used to hang above their round beds. In the photo, Joan wears a pink suit and the dull smile of a terminally ill toddler. Her skin is thickly smeared with makeup, and above her eyes are the two winged Roman chariots (mastodon tusks, Iroquois canoes) she used for eyebrows.

She outlines for us her way of life: her busy, busy day of being *not* a has-been; how to mix Belgians, bearded painters, and hairdressers for a perfect cocktail party; not putting red food next to yellow food because it looks unappetizing to her; and settles once and for all the debate about whether to use whole eggs or just yolks to add shine to your hair (it's the whole egg). She explains how she works exercise into her busy life, how she'll sometimes pause in doorways and just place her palms against the top and push herself down into the floor with all her might, or how she keeps her hips strong by scooting across her floor an ass cheek at a time. She tells you how to get your maid to properly stuff the sleeves of your Chanel suits, and that the best way to learn a new word every day is to use it in a sentence. (Incidentally, when you start doing that is when you know you're doomed.) She tells us a little about "Mamacita," the nickname she gave her maid, who was German, not that it mattered, and the mother of one of Joan's friends who had no problem pimping her out to a movie star. Joan recalls the first time Mamacita was "brought over" to audition at housecleaning and how she hired her when she saw that, instead of using a bucket and mop, the old woman went "handsies, kneesies" on the floor. (It's the only way to really get into the corners and thus Joan warmed to her instantly.) I knew Joan wasn't any "great lady," and anyone who admired her so should not be trusted.

The minutes before the start of the evening's classes were the stillest, the only sound coming when the massive front door swung open and heralded a noisy gust of boulevard along with another girl bumping her big dance bag into the foyer.

Who would it be? Would it be intimidating Cathy, to dazzle us with her three Shakespearean speeches, maybe in a Southern accent even? Or the Czechs, all tawny and calm, their foreheads encircled with bandannas? It might be wayward, freckly Christine, Dorothy's pet project, except that Christine seemed to always be there already. (She may have actually lived there.) Perhaps it would be Cathy's little buddy Mona, of the spindly limbs and giant, sloshing soda cup? Or please, please, God, make it be Frizzy Sheri or some other newish girl toward whom I could feel a smug superiority and therefore do my best work. My neck was getting full with worms, my stomach now a block of rust, enslithered by intestines of eels, black shiny electric eels with glass-button eyes and mouths agape.

I'd glimpse Dorothy buzzing around, doing whatever she did as the Academy administrator. Besides collecting the tuitions and presiding over the filing cabinet where the scenes were kept, it seemed her most important job was to set a paper plate of Cheese Nips on the stage before the acting lessons started. Yet somehow, she always forgot to do it, thus rousing the ire of Francis, the Academy director.

Francis Lederer was a Czech actor so old and obscure, even old and obscure people were unaware of him. My mother swore she remembered him, but later agreed to the possibility that she may have been thinking of Rod La Rocque. He was a romantic leading man type, and did lots of European theater, wartime German cinema (like *The Wonderful Lies of Nina Petrovna*—have you seen it? He played Gerd) and is said to have done a short stint on *That Girl,* although it remains undocumented. Regardless, his was just the kind of omnibus that really impressed adolescent girls in the eighties.

He was still very tall, and still very old (very, very old), and moved with the erect assurance of a man who'd come to Los Angeles in the orange grove days and had the good sense to buy up the portions of the San Fernando Valley that didn't already belong to Bob Hope. He wore the same clothes every day: short-sleeved parchment-white whisper-thin dress shirt with machine-embroidered flourish down

the front, mud brown trousers, and mud brown orthopedic shoes with roomy toe boxes sloped like the ears of
hounds. I guess you can get away with that sort of thing
when you are the honorary mayor of Canoga Park.

He'd survey the room, pausing to smile in a weird Slavic
way, or glare at someone, or raise his finger slowly and
even more slowly shake it, deciding whether or not to say
what he was thinking or just let that student wonder. (Let
wonder, usually.) If the Czechs were in house, he'd have
long, giddy exchanges with them in their native tongue,
which made everyone else feel very safe and included.

Inevitably there would be something wrong. He'd bel-
low out for Dorothy in the loudest Czechoslovakian theater
voice you'd ever heard, "Mzzzzzz Barrrretttttt!!!" In she'd
scurry, a blur of bows and checks, and stop short, curtsy,
splay her fingers beneath her chin, flutter her eyelashes, and
say, "Yes, sir, Mr. Lederer, sir?" on the off, off chance that
this excessive self-degradation could suddenly turn endear-
ing, just this one time.

This was probably a holdover from her chorus days
back in the Past, most notably as one of the ladies in *The
Wizard of Oz* who assists with Dorothy Gale's Emerald
City makeover in the "Snip snip here, snip snip there, and
a couple of tra la las" scene. I'm not certain, but she might
be the one who replies "Mmmm hmmm!" when Dorothy
asks, "Can you even dye my eyes to match my gown?"
which, coincidentally, messed with my mind almost as
much as the acid queen scene with the iron maiden of
syringes in *Tommy* did when I saw it as a child. The thought
of having one's eyes dyed by a group of strangers while

lying on a metal plank is petrifying. How would they *dye her eyes* to match her gown? Jolly old town, my ass.

The curtsy and the eyelash batting would infuriate Francis to the point where he became unable to look anywhere near her during the scolding.

"Would it be possible, Mzzzzzzzzz Barrettt," he'd ask, arms crossed, face a tangle of hate, "to put a plate of something on the stage [this part growing louder and louder and accentuated with one foot stamp per syllable] ONCE AND FOR ALL?"

"Yes, sir, Mr. Lederer! Right away, sir!" and with that she'd turn on her musical-comedy heels and be off, returning, always, when Francis was in the middle of a sentence, with a plate of Cheese Nips that she'd tiptoe into place. "Next time, please spare all of us and yourself this embarrassment" was all he'd manage to say, to the floor.

It was as if you were watching Bette Davis's character Baby Jane Hudson in *What Ever Happened to Baby Jane?* come to life and interact with Hannibal Lecter. Then, cast them both in an imaginary version of *Who's Afraid of Virginia Woolf?* and you'll have some idea what we mild-hearted teen and preteen girls were made to witness whenever something like the temperature needed adjusting, or there weren't enough chairs, or a student was missing. And then, should anyone ever ask you, say, who *is* afraid of Virginia Woolf and what *did* ever happen to Baby Jane? you'll know the answers: "I am," and "This."

The Academy wasn't an actual school like the one on *Fame*. There was no English teacher stressing the importance of scholastic achievement over the inconsistencies of show business and constantly butting heads with the kid who thinks that reading "The Rime of the Ancient Mariner" and all that book learning is just bullshit and a waste of his time because dance is all that matters and dance will be his ticket out of the ghetto, while a dance teacher tells the English teacher to back off and stop undermining everyone's dreams, and eventually school property gets vandalized and everyone feels the heat.

Even though I spent twenty hours a week at the Academy, I still had to go to regular eighth grade.

I was just reentering the Los Angeles public school system after busing, the experimental and remarkably unpopular program wherein kids from the public schools in affluent areas (honkies) were taken on very long bus rides every day to impoverished inner city schools to spread good cheer, and vice versa.

The three years of busing were, coincidentally, the three years I spent in a tiny, adobe-style, midpriced private school, where circumstances had led to such things as my first Porsche ride (Keri Berg's dad took us for pizza) and everyone worked toward similar goals. It was deep in the Valley and it was called Valley School. Their motto was "Valley School: in the heart of the Valley."

But now they had drop-kicked me into the minimum-security prison that was Robert A. Millikan Junior High. It was like having a tidal wave crash in my intestines every hour on the hour. The kids I remembered from the days before busing were either gone, dead, or unrecognizable. Where were all the other whiteys, working toward similar goals? I could only linger in the social perimeter, since I was the only student who knew much about the repertoire of Joel Grey. All at once, I was awash in a sea of complicated surnames and hostile burritos.

During lunch it was on the outermost bench I'd be, brown bag (peanut butter and jelly, Granny Goose chips, Capri Sun drink bag) on my lap with my one friend, Vicky Goodhead. How she and I came together is lost to history, but it was our mutual smallness, whiteness, and sullen faces that kept us together, every day, on that bench.

It's hard to know which is more tragic—that she was named Vicky Goodhead, or that when roll was called each morning and everyone snickered, I thought to myself, "Okay, people, give it a rest already. So she has a 'good head' on her shoulders. It's not *that* funny. Jeez!" Vicky resembled Diane Chambers, Shelley Long's character on *Cheers.* She had the same pyramid of blond hair, wore the same feminine sweaters, but her expression was different. Her face looked like the result of a tragic nap, one where she fell asleep, for whatever reason, with the crown of her head resting against a hot oven, making certain features wilt downward ever so slightly.

As the days went on, Vicky grew ever glummer, until she was not much more than a pile of rags around a Jantzen book bag. I was a different kind of girl: tortured by internal serpents in public, but quite at ease in small, safe groups (of one to three). I could even be quite a ham with lots of opinions and a downright wicked streak. It wasn't completely out of character for me to draw an unflattering picture of someone on his locker for a laugh, I enjoyed talking some shit, and I wasn't shy about making what I saw as worth-while crank calls, or shouting rude things at strangers who drove by my house.

"Did you see *America's Funniest Bloopers* last night?" was something I might ask Vicky to inspire conversation. "There was a goat that bit a guy in the butt. It was pretty good."

But Vicky would barely engage me. Mostly, we two just hovered above our brown bags, next to our book bags, staring off at dim gray spots on the ground that used to be gum.

Her name was Vicky Goodhead, I may have mentioned.

"So why didn't you join the drama club?" you must be asking, "and make friends with those losers?" Well, I wasn't supposed to. When you studied at the Academy, you were discouraged from having any other dramatic instruction that might muddy the fountain of your impressionable mind. That was the way it had to be. At the Academy, you per-formed the same scenes over and over again, but sometimes you'd use a Southern accent. Performing in *Bye Bye Birdie* under the direction of a junior high drama teacher would be to risk developing the wrong brain muscles, and then I'd be fucked. Besides, the drama club kids were lamer than lame. I wasn't about to hang around with the likes of Danny Nucci in his white T-shirt, vest, and bowler hat.

"Got a problem, Laura Ingalls? Do you miss Pa?"

This was Tina Chastain talking, and making everybody on the bleachers laugh during P.E. I was sitting out due to a groin pull of the modern jazz variety, and she and her friends were sitting out because they had just lit some Marlboro Lights and it would have been a shame to put them out.

"Why aren't you on the prairie, bitch?"

Something about me reminded Tina of Laura Ingalls from *Little House on the Prairie*.

"Did Manly hump you too hard last night?" she asked, referring to the nickname Laura Ingalls Wilder gave her husband, Almanzo. This made everyone laugh and laugh and laugh.

Tina Chastain was a rough little lady. I'm not sure if she actually went to Robert A. Millikan Junior High School. She was one of those kids whose picture wasn't in the yearbook, because, for whatever reason, she just couldn't make it on picture day. She'd disappear for long stretches of time, and then just be sitting there in homeroom, looking as if she was dealing with some heavy shit. I'd heard something about her being found living with some runaways on Hollywood Boulevard. She seemed to move between worlds without much fuss. Sometimes I wondered if I was the only person who could actually see her.

Her head, her whole body, really, looked like a minitruck. Mint green and charcoal pinstripes would not have been out of place running the length of her sides, which they could've easily done as there was no separation between her head, shoulders, trunk, legs, or feet—she was just one block of genderless wrath. Her face had that mashed-in Phil Collins look, wherein both mouth and eyes are indicated by angry little piecrust slits and separated by broad cheeks the color of ham. Her hair was a cap of tight ash blond curls that she kept ever dewy by the liberal use of a gelatinous product called Dep. She was an angel just flown up from hell.

"Do you have a fucking problem?" asked her friend Winnie, who would, in later years, sell me Actifed cold medicine and tell me it was speed. "What's your problem?"

Me? No problem. Just sittin' here thinking about Robert Preston, is all.

"You'd better get back to the prairie."

In a way, I am already there, actually. We are all of us on our own personal—

"Did you have sex on the prairie last night? Did Pa finger-fuck you in your little prairie house?"

No. I don't think so. Nothing like that. Please stop laughing, all of you.

It didn't matter what was actually happening, Tina could find an occasion for humiliation. If there was a shark on a page of a biology text, she'd say, "Is that what your daddy looks like?" which left me more confused than anything— was she comparing the actor Michael Landon to the shark, or my biological father, Vic Grenrock? Was I not Laura Ingalls at that point?

Bullies were new to me. I'd had run-ins with other kids, but things were always on equal footing. Before Robert A. Millikan Junior High, and the predominance of, among other things, unitards in my life, I had attained a respectable standing among children and preteens—I'd worn puka shells in school pictures only a year before this. My hair had frontal quadrant feathers to rival anyone's; stiff, auburn shingles, they were, flanking the typical sly and silver-bracketed smile of youth. I'd lingered long and mellow in the pot haze, I'd worn the woven poncho, eaten the mini–cheese cubes. I knew things.

Most of the kids at Millikan still had some form of feathering to their hair, were still listening to Journey, and Mexican ponchos were still their cover-up of choice for the cool Southern California mornings, but it had been time for me to put away stonerish things. I had let my feathers grow away down my shoulders and reclaimed the hairstyle God had intended for me: long, obdurate waves with a garland of frizz marking the hairline. ("Saturday Night Shtetl," I call it.) I'd pull the top portion back to keep it out of my eyes, and because, when acting, Francis needed to be able to see your face. Knowing what I do of the junior high student's limited catalog of references, I think this is what made me look like Laura Ingalls from *Little House on the Prairie* to Tina (although in truth, my hair was closer in style to that of Mary's, the older sister).

Many kids would've cracked at this point. Never mind Black Sabbath and Grand Theft Auto—the effect of Joan Crawford's intimate musings on the benefits of a glass of buttermilk at bedtime might have on the underformed teenaged frontal lobe (where impulse control is stored), combined with unfair taunting at school, is more than enough to cause one to take to one's trench coat. Any book with sentences like "I hesitate when it comes to chintz" and "How I adore pink!" should come with a parental advisory sticker. Thank God I had early the influence of Bowie lyrics about moving like tigers on Vaseline to even me out or I would have probably been one of those kids who opens fire in the cafeteria.

I think the idea was that I looked too, too pure for this junior high. Robert A. Millikan Junior High didn't deserve me, quite honestly. Especially physical education classes, from which the necessary paperwork was in the process of excusing me for good. I had just become aware of a little-known provision in the L.A. Unified School District rules and regulations: if a student completed a certain amount of hours of extracurricular physical education per week (like, if you were Olympics-bound, or did a lot of tap routines to Andrews Sisters songs), then that student got to skip P.E. and go home early and watch *General Hospital*. I was a serious dancer, so track, flag football, or volleyball were indelicate pursuits that could coarsen the swanlike arch of my foot, or distend my little marble-hard thighs (not to exceed the calf in diameter), and if that were to happen, I'd have to be taken out back and shot. Besides, you couldn't *port de bras* with volleyball wrists, now could you?

A few summers before, my old friend Linda (of the *All That Jazz* soundtrack, who had not escaped busing and was attending a different junior high) and I had nursed adjacent crushes on singer/actor Rick Springfield. We went to his concert at the Universal Amphitheater, sat in the orchestra pit, and recounted for months afterward every event leading up to the moment when Rick jumped off the stage midsong, ran down the row of chairs in front of us, and christened us with a spray of his teen-idol, mismatched-Converse-wearing, Australian working-class-dog sweat. Oh, how we recalled it, over and over again. We joined the fan club, put up posters, sang his songs, recalled it some more, loved him deeply, and, after school resumed, still managed to get together to reminisce about the events of that summer, as Linda's schedule permitted (what was she always doing? I was the busy one, and I always made time!). She didn't seem all that excited when I told her the great news that I would be going home early enough to catch most of Rick Springfield as Dr. Noah Drake on *General Hospital*. It got to be that I could barely get her on the phone to give her the daily Rick report ("knit tie, beige plaid shirt, lab coat, kissed the gross blonde, lips looked very pink"). I mean, I didn't have to do that—I saw it. It's sad what jealousy can do to a person.

I also adored a character played by Emma Samms called Holly Sutton. I thought she was the most beautiful, lovely English rose in all the rose garden. She had doll cheeks that looked like they had been buffed smooth from the White Cliffs of Dover by local craftsmen. She always had a look of earnest, sometimes tearful yearning. I yearned to yearn as Holly yearned. When she looked at someone for whom she felt a yearning, her eyes went right-left-right-left, and her little English rosebud mouth simpered downward, away from her soft brown tubes of hair, which were anchored heavenward on the sides by unseen combs. They dressed her in shimmering rust or burgundy things that my mother calls "blouses" tucked into high-waisted, heavy skirts from which knee-high boots emerged. Her lipstick always matched her "blouse" and I loved her. Francis talked a lot about facial bone structure, and Emma Samms's was perfect. Even though she was from another storyline, I felt she was the perfect woman for Rick Springfield to yearn for and love and hold and be warm and brown and earnest with.

Under my bed I kept a big watercolor pad with a blueprint of the penthouse apartment I was designing for her/me (the fusion of whom was an actress-being called "Anastasia") at the most cosmopolitan place I could think of: the top floor of Bonaventure Hotel. You may know it as the four black glass cylinders with exterior glass elevators that the makers of montages always include as an authentic L.A. sight, or maybe as the fictional setting for the 1980s Ann Jillian sitcom *It's a Living,* about the waitresses and piano player who always acted like a prick.

I designed the fantasy penthouse in a half-circle because, given the limitations of a daytime-drama salary, I deduced that someone else certainly inhabited the other side (that's always been the thing about my fantasies, they're just realistic enough to be heartbreaking).

Echoing the half-circle premise, I based much of the interior on a shell design. The furniture was mostly white satin or mauve suede. There was mauve carpet and I was thinking of doing the walls in either light mauve or mauve. The white satin bed had an upholstered cover that opened up like a clamshell. I/she could leave it open or closed during the day—I designed it to look good either way. It wasn't until years later that I actually went to the Bonaventure Hotel and rode the big glass outward-facing elevator up to the top, which was not a penthouse, but a revolving bar full of snazzily dressed Korean teens.

That was my fantasy for home. My fantasy for school hours went like this: I'd be sitting there in class (maybe with odd little Mr. Jacobs, who taught math from the perspective of a character of his own invention called "Dilcue"—the inversion of "Euclid"—who did everything wrong, mathwise), and a student messenger would enter and interrupt. Mr. Jacobs would look up and call for Stacey Grenrock, and I would respond, my faint voice cracking just a little. He would tell me that there was an important call for me and I needed to go to the office. I'd go to the office and take the call. It would be Francis calling me out of school on some business! Some important acting business!

The point of the fantasy was that a powerful person from that world was rescuing me from this world, and everyone in this world would be really impressed, and the ones who were not would at least be intrigued. They'd want to know about this person, this "Stacey" with the phone call. What was her powerful extracurricular life? Who were its players? Tina Chastain would get wind of it and just fall forward into her tub of Dep, which would serve to muffle her sobs. She'd be suddenly overcome with shame for herself. She'd scurry for some fig leaves or a Jantzen book bag to cover her four-wheel-drive nakedness, and I would float out of Robert A. Millikan Junior High School early that day, unconcerned.

"Darlink-k-k-k?" If Francis stared at you and said this, it was your cue to recite your repertoire.

There were seven scenes: one from Lillian Hellman's play *The Children's Hour*, which we all performed faithfully, never having a clue that it was about a couple of lezzies; *This Property Is Condemned* (Tennessee Williams), in which one girl got to play crazy; *Teach Me How to Cry* (no idea, but it seemed to be about a nasty girl and a nice girl); *The Bad Seed*, which no one wanted to do because it required one of us to play a boy, or act with a boy, of which there were few. (For a short time we had one who was the very young Eurasian son of the very old American actor Robert Cummings. He had an obsession with the Czechs that made people uncomfortable.) The very advanced and slightly older stars were allowed to do scenes from the adult class, like the hard-core Cockney teen pregnancy mother/daughter anguish of *A Taste of Honey,* a bitchy scene from *The Women,* and, males permitting, some light comedy from *Who's Afraid of Virginia Woolf?*

Those are the scenes we did, the only scenes we did, ever. Over, and over, and over again, no others, but sometimes we did them with a Southern accent.

Francis watched carefully and stopped us every time it appeared that we were "just saying lines." Often he stressed each syllable of direction with a stamp of his hound brown orthopedic shoe. Have you ever seen a skunk stamp his little paws to stand his ground? It wasn't cute like that. It was like this: "Darlink, you have got to got to got to got to . . . (*stamp stamp stamp stamp, stamp stamp stamp stamp* . . .) speak louder so that we can hear you hear you hear you . . ."

There was also "Do something, do something, do something!" which was your signal to replay the scene and this time, for God's sake, eat from the provided plate of Cheese Nips. A performance he strongly disliked was "to vomit!" If he asked you a question and you didn't answer him clearly enough, he'd let you know by squirming around in his chair and making a mocking, nasally sound like "whawhawhawha?" And if you really weren't getting it, he'd call for "Katarina the Great" to come up and recite to you one of the sayings on the plaques (when necessary, as Mae West).

My fellow stars and I were fresh off a stellar stage performance at that weekend's annual Youth in Entertainment awards at the Mayfair Theater, so you could say we were feeling pretty good. From their inception in 1979, the Youthies, as they are probably not really called, were designed to honor excellence by young adults in film, TV, miniseries, movies of the week, after-school specials, and theater. Youthies are still given out, but now Young Hollywood just has the statues forwarded to their suites at the Palms in Vegas, where they are ground into a fine dust and sprinkled over the homeless amid a chorus of sharp cackling. But back in '81, we still knew how to put on a *show*. We stars, in our *Chorus Line* top hats, sparkly vests, canes, bow ties, smiles, black tights, high-heeled tap shoes (and in my case, a gut of solid eels—writhing, cold, and oily), performed a dance number to Neil Diamond's Dixieland classic "The Robert E. Lee." Why? Ours was not to wonder why, ours was just to tap or die.

The previous year, Quinn Cummings from *The Goodbye Girl* and the show *Family* had really swept the Youthies. She was supposed to be the current litmus test for what casting directors who cast children prized most: personality. "Look at that personality!" all the mothers would say. All the kids were encouraged to project personality. It was a word that always made me shudder, because I knew I had none.

This year was supposed to be Sydney Penny's year. She had enough personality to be the most nominated for best young actress (*The Patricia Neal Story*, *The Capture of Grizzly*

Adams, The Circle Family) but she ended up losing each time to Nancy McKeon for the special *Please Don't Hit Me, Mom* and *The Facts of Life Goes to Paris*. You just never could tell how things might go.

Francis fixed his gaze on Sheri, the poor mush-brown-haired girl whose head looked like a tilted egg upon a hunchbacked, dirty body. Her protruding throat was in constant swallow and her eyes were always damp and dim. Her ankles and wrists were too small for the rest of her, which gave her limbs a weird, tapered look and her dancing a real gutless quality. But worst of all, she had a high, whiny voice, which she could hardly get to an acceptable stage volume—inspiring endless "whawhawhawha's" from Francis. Mom and I would sometimes make each other laugh on the ride home by singing that old song "Sherrrrrrrriiiiiiiii, Sherrrriiiii ba-a-by" because the singer sounded just like her!

It was mean, but funny!

Sheri rattled off the few measly scenes that she knew, and Francis, like it was nothing at all, like it happened every day, spoke but one word: *"Picnic!"*

Picnic? *Picnic* was the ultimate insult, a baby scene—the first one you learned and never did again. The others, give or take, were good, substantial scenes—there was no shame in *Children's Hour,* save for the required solemn reiteration of the arcane insults "goose" and "fibber." No, to perform *Picnic* was torture, especially in the lesser role of Madge, who basically just looks up from her needlepoint and says, "You look very pretty," and then cocks her head with concern for the rest of the scene. Francis was obviously sending Sheri a message. And guess who was to be her Madge. He'd never do that to Cathy, or the Czechs. Maybe Christine, never Mona. I must've displeased him somehow.

He spent nearly half the class torturing Sheri, which was fine, but I didn't get to do any other scenes. For a closer, Cathy was called upon to do some Shakespeare— no accent.

Tuesdays and Fridays went like this: two hours of acting, an hour of jazz, an hour of ballet, dinner/remorse break, half an hour of tap, followed by "speech," a fifteen-minute, often ditched, Dorothy-led class tacked on at the end. (Saturdays had a different schedule and a strict color scheme.) She hated to be left out, and felt it was her duty to mark the Tuesday and Friday students, stars included, with her invaluable gingham-scented urine. Here's what I remember Dorothy teaching us in "speech": she taught us how to enunciate by having us enunciate the word "enunciate" again and again, and she taught us that you can only part your hair in the middle if you have a turned-up nose—otherwise, no middle part.

I spent most of my pre-, early-, and middle adolescence in those rooms, doubting, plotting, fearing, cackling, crying, scrutinizing, worrying, and aching.

And when it was over, I got to have chicken strips.

At ten o'clock every Tuesday and Friday night, when normal kids were off huffing paint and learning social skills, my parents would pick me up from the Academy and on the way home, we'd stop at Pioneer Chicken. There were Kentucky Fried Chicken families, and there were Pioneer Chicken families, and we were a Pioneer family.

Pioneer families were a much, much smaller group, and it wasn't until I grew up that I realized that, among chicken eaters, Pioneer is considered real bottom-of-the-fryer stuff, just slightly fancier than gristle, a bit more substantive than salt pork. The crispity-crunchity crust was an emboldened orange, the flesh bespoke short lives of mute misery, yet we would sooner carve swastikas on our foreheads than let even one of the Colonel's eleven herbs and spices pass our lips.

I'm not sure why, since both chicken joints (all chicken joints) were and are disgusting, but I think it was probably because my mom didn't like Colonel Sanders's whole vibe. She probably sensed something oppressive and right-wing emitting from him, whereas Pioneer Pete was a jolly cartoon character who smiled from his covered wagon and would never deny you your right to a safe and legal abortion. I'll bet he'd even bring over some chicken when you were all done and back at home. I don't suspect Sanders would have done that. There was just something extra wicked about him. I'm so glad he's dead.

Esteban was always working on those nights. I can still see him lolling over the deep fryers in the empty restaurant, his diminutive frame barely holding up his orange polyester Pioneer uniform, his face going from dazed indifference to slight recognition when he saw us. I'd go to the counter, my peach unitard slippery under street clothes, my bloodless face glazed with dried sweat, my hairline now a stiffer garland of frizz, and place my order. My order never varied: "Strips 'n' Chips with mashed potatoes, please." Strips 'n' Chips was the intended combo, but instead of "chips"

(French fries—as if we were in Britain), I'd substitute a small side of mashed potatoes. A meal of two different types of deep-fried stick just seemed gauche, so I ordered off the menu.

After about a year, Esteban really came to expect our twice-weekly visits. Sometimes he'd even chime in at the last bit: "with mashed potatoes!" and we'd all laugh. Once, my dad tried to place the order *en español*. What a disaster! Esteban always put my order together, all the while shooting me wild-eyed glances, as if he couldn't believe I was there just for chicken and nothing more.

Starved, I'd have to devour at least one strip and scrape away the canopy of stabilized mashed potato gravy in the car. Dancing and self-doubt really work up an appetite in a growing girl, and I needed sustenance at regular intervals. Once, the competing acids in my stomach had me writhing around on the floor in such pain that only after the dispensation of small mouthfuls of 7 Up and drugstore pound cake was I able to stand up and carry on tapping. I could recall only a circle of confused leg warmers around my contorting body for what seemed like the longest time.

Back at home, I'd dance that evening's routines better than I could ever do in class. Only in the safety of my family room, in the black and copper womb where the little lamb did pronk, could I really let go and put my hip into it. I could never do that in class. I could never really put my hip into it.

Saturdays at the Academy were altogether different.

They started with a very early class called "Song Interpretation," taught by Francis for only the most precious and talented students. It was possible to be adored by him and a member of all his classes but still not be privileged enough to act out songs in Song Interpretation. I'll never forget when I was finally asked. I didn't sleep the entire night before (or after, for about twenty years), and my voice trembled so much I barely made it through the first verse of "Goody Goody!"

Cathy, Ingrid and Karin, and both their mothers worked at the Academy on Saturdays so that they could be on scholarship. I wanted to be on scholarship, too, so, even though we could afford the classes, I made my mother work there on Saturdays. It was strategy, really, but my mom thought of it as scrubbing toilets and implied that Dorothy could be "disrespectful to her and the other mothers." I know what you might be thinking, but don't go shedding any tears for ol' Charlotte Grenrock. She got something out of it, too: the right to shout, "I scrubbed TOILETS for you!" in all future lectures to me. Besides, she only did it like one time.

Saturday was also different because that's when Dorothy's little ones came. They had to wear the Academy colors: red and black. The girls wore red gingham shifts with black tights, and boys wore red gingham shirts and black jazz pants. All the little ones were taught three basic things: a simple tap routine to "Tea for Two," a simple tap routine to "By the Sea," and to stay the fuck away from Francis.

Every so often there was one who stood out. Some of my readers might remember the little fellow with the big beige

Afro who danced in Deniece Williams's "Let's Hear It for the Boy" video. That was tiny Aaron. He had so much personality, and we all marveled at the way he projected it.

We stars were severely outnumbered on Saturdays, but there were still enough of us to have our own special classes away from Dorothy and her gingham child soldiers. We were counted on to continue the red and black tradition, but we often strayed. This infuriated Dorothy, and since I was about the youngest and smallest of the special ones, she tried to trick me into wearing a gingham shift when I started coming on Saturdays.

"Yes, everyone has to wear these on Saturdays," she said, poking through a rack of those little red dresses in her lady-sized red gingham shift over black polyester adult pants. "Here's one that'll fit you. Put it on." Nice try, asshole. I guess I must've looked like some kind of sucker to her.

We mostly wore black unitards and red sweatshirts on Saturdays, but occasionally, someone would throw in some magenta or peach, just to fuck with her. What was she going to do? We were untouchable, we Stars of the Academy.

The only time all the ages came together was for a fifteen-minute lecture called Career Guidance. This was where Francis tried to give everyone advice about the careers they might someday have, using insider tales about Claudette Colbert and Beverly Sills to illustrate his points (although one time, he just had Nancy perform the "Black Widow" song for the full fifteen minutes). He once made us swear an oath that we would never touch drugs or alcohol and that we would never behave in a way that would get us a reputation for being difficult. I adhered to only one of these tenents.

Lately, all this career advice was particularly useful for me, because soon, I'd be getting my own headshots.

My parents used to bring our new dog Sandy to the local park early every morning. They had developed a regular little dog club with a few other folks with dogs who brought them to the park early in the morning. There were my parents and Sandy; a very old lady named Mary and her dog, Blarney; Lee Colomby—the mother of Scott Colomby, who played the sleeveless caddy Denunzio in *Caddyshack*—and her dog Champers; and a middle-aged guy named Russell who didn't actually have a dog. Lee was a former stage actress who had just downshifted into child agentry and gotten a job at a highly unregarded agency in Burbank. It was decided that I was to be represented by her. It seemed like a great thing: I'd be the beneficiary of all that concentrated Colomby power, what with Scott set to star in *Porky's II: The Next Day,* and the father about to direct a new TV pilot called *Report to Murphy,* starring a promising new talent known then as Michael Keaton.

(Most people don't know I've met Michael Keaton. I don't talk about it much, but I remember it like it was 1982: Lee Colomby took me to the set of *Report to Murphy,* a comedy about an overworked parole officer named Murphy. It was only the pilot, so there was that hopeful feeling in the air. After it was over, I met Lee's husband, and next to him was the star of the show. His shirtsleeves were still in parole-officer roll from shooting. Lee said, "Michael, this is Stacey. Stacey, this is Michael Keaton." He shook my hand, firmly but softly, two qualities that can coexist in stars, and said, "Hello, Stacey. It is nice to meet you," and that is exactly how it happened.)

The first order of business was to get a proper headshot and composite. Lee Colomby set me up with an established child photographer, a woman named Lynn who worked from her home in the Valley. Lynn told my mother to bring lots of outfits for lots of different activities I'd be pretending to like doing in these photos. On one side was to be a matte-finish eight-by-ten headshot, and on the other, a composite of shots composed in a visually expected manner (usually one in each corner with a nice oval inset dead center) of the subject (me) in action. Of course, this was so casting directors, directors, and producers could picture you in a variety of roles. The idea is to make it as easy as possible for the governing forces to hire you.

The whole system is designed so the producer (we'll call him Garry Marshall for simplicity's sake) has to do as little brain-thinking as possible. Imagine our fictional producer, Garry Marshall, needs to cast a young lady in a show called *Laverne & Shirley*, starring his sister, the fabricated Penny Marshall. The bulk of *Laverne & Shirley*'s action takes place in Milwaukee in the 1950s. Imagine you are a young lady up for the guest-starring role of Emily, Shirley's rambunctious, starry-eyed backwoods cousin. If you had a picture of yourself sipping a malted and wearing a poodle skirt on your composite, you'd be in much better shape than a young actress who chose instead to depict herself rototilling, money-laundering, goose-stepping, pulling taffy, in a root cellar, collating papers, etc.

The problem is, there is no way in hell an actor can ever hope to predict what Garry is looking for. You trust that Garry will hire a casting director who can use a reasonable amount of imagination to picture what one might look like as a taffy puller, with taffy in fists, pulling it. But no, Garry won't (hence the people who wear lab coats to audition for the role of doctor), and this is why everyone who tries to act professionally will end up strapped to a metal slab in a facility on the outskirts of town, asking the attendants if they can even dye her eyes to match her gown.

Lynn suggested we bring wardrobe that was born from "things I like to do." She left it up to us. What did I like to do? I liked to daydream. Make an origami version of a plate of Cheese Nips and place it on my desk so it would always be there. I liked to design penthouses for people who didn't exist. I liked to sit in my room alone, singing "Delta Dawn." I liked to steal my father's jar of rubber cement and use it to fuse the backs of my ears to my head. Would those be good things to photograph?

We, of course, consulted Dorothy, and she unearthed for us a country-style cotton dress that had been used in some bullshit Academy Christmas pageant thing or other. It was maize yellow, with tiny little wildflowers and a black rick-rack border. There were buttons to the neck, and a little black ribbon to tie when you got there, and a tiny pocket for keeping Indian head pennies, and wishes. When I put it on, I looked well suited to stand outside the general store with my fellow townsfolk as we all shat ourselves over the impending arrival of the Wells Fargo wagon.

Not only that, this was the second time I had been type-cast as frontiersy. There was the Pennzoil industrial film I did at age three, where I played the darling young girl buying penny candy in the general store. I knew there was no escaping what I was. Still, I don't know why everyone wanted to put me on the prairie.

We cobbled together a few more things—my new Levi's, a darling little powder blue boat-necked sweater, seersucker shorts, a Victorian lace top that I wish I still had, white tights (for the dress), doll-style Chinese slippers, a Hawaiian shirt, and puka shells from my old life, a cherry red and purple island-flower rayon skirt I had made that summer in sewing class to wear to my new school, a painter's cap, dancewear, and a batch of pastel bandannas.

We got the crucial headshot (for which I wore the Victorian top) out of the way first. Lynn cheered me along so that my smile would "really pop!" My eyes needed to jump off the page. That was how you got auditions. Something in your eyes needed to jump off the casting director's desk and grab her by the throat and choke her a little.

The sun caught my garland of hairline frizz and got lost in it. My smile was goofy, so goofy, and my pre-tweezed, preteen eyebrows, bereft of any discernible arch, looked not like Joan Crawford's majestic pair of king cobras, poised for attack, but more like a pair of immigrant grandparents who sit every night in their sweat-sheened recliners, and about whom you feel a good deal of shame.

On to the prairie dress. Lynn thought the best way to

showcase this "darling" wardrobe would be to have me do some apple picking. My job was to look delighted and project my personality and jump off the page and really pop as I held up the prop apple and stood on a ladder near a tree. I was to do this again as I hula-hooped, and then tied my roller skates for the next shots. Lynn used all her child photographer tricks to "bring me out" and "make it look real," but I just ended up looking surprised, and like a terminally ill toddler.

I had a photography book when I was a kid called *Scavullo Women* (I had seen it on a morning show and made my mother take me to the mall to buy it that day). It's photographs of women, mostly famous, taken by the famous ascot-and-sailor-hat-wearing photographer Francesco Scavullo. Scavullo said something in the Rita Coolidge section (that I'm sure I was only reading because I had read the Brooke Shields and Gia Carangi chapters to death) that went something like this: "It was the end of the day, and Rita had wiped off her makeup and brushed out her hair, and I thought she was the most beautiful thing I'd ever seen. I said, Don't go anywhere, and I took this picture." And there was a picture of Rita Coolidge looking like whatever Rita Coolidge looked like but with her hair down. (Photographers and makeup artists always pretend not to see a difference between models and, for example, their elderly mothers, or folk singers, or some weird old Yugoslavian princess whom no one has ever heard of. There is a difference, and they know it.) Scavullo was saying that that was when he and Rita got real and let themselves be artists. I've since, in my entertainment travels, seen this moment unfold numerous times: the end-of-the-day shot. I've seen Elizabeth Berkley from *Showgirls* just forget all the bullshit and have fun with it. It's a magic moment, and it happened between Lynn and me.

"Let's have some fun now." She winked. As much as I'd love to say she sent my mother away and forced me to take my top off through the tears that signaled the end of my innocence, that's not what happened. What did happen is far worse: Lynn dressed me up like a little Jackie Coogan–style street urchin, with a dirty shirt, newsboy cap, and cheek smudge. My parents still have this picture on a shelf and every time I walk past it, I hate myself in a new way.

The Hamburger Hamlet restaurant on Van Nuys Boulevard in Sherman Oaks was, to me, awash in the kind of candle-y yellow, intellectual glaze that glowed from the screen during Woody Allen movies. It was dark and had deep green leather-like booths and modern-art-museum posters in thin silver frames, but in addition to that, it had a bawdy Elizabethan theme. For example, the side dishes on the menu were under the heading "Eat the Sides, I Pray You." To me, it was Elaine's. In my mind, it played host to mainly a theater crowd (but I probably thought that because the General Cinemas were across the street). I thought Marsha Mason and Neil Simon probably went there and shared a plate of the Hamlet staple called "Those Potatoes" and quipped things to each other, reveling in middle age, and maybe, what the hell, sending a slice of cheesecake over to Jill Clayburgh, who sat silken-bloused and alone in a corner booth. She'd glance up from her copy of *The White*

Hotel and raise her pale hand in a gesture of acknowledgment in their direction.

My dad and I ended up there one Sunday afternoon after we had dropped off all my pictures at the printer. After much trepidation, my agent, my parents, and I had selected the shots that popped (which in spirit could be titled "Churlish Ragamuffin," "Everybody's Apple-Eating Confidante," "Hey, You're Awful Cute for an Orchard Hand," "I'd Love to Skate with You—Just Let Me Get These Skates Tied," and "Who'd-a-Thought? Me, Stacey Grenrock! Hula-Hooping!"). I had chosen a font for the print called "Olive Antique Italic," which I thought suited me well: I was a little olive, a little antique, and altogether italicized.

I ordered a cheeseburger with "those little fried onions" and a mug's worth of frosty beer of root. Dad ordered a comparable entrée, and a beer.

But Francis said never to drink.

"Oh," Dad said. "Is that right?"

"Yes," I said, and I told him all the ways alcohol would make people talk badly of you and ruin your career.

He tried to explain to me that he only ever had a beer every now and then, but that kind of thing is a losing battle by definition. It's like calling someone a "suspected rapist," or walking up to someone and saying, "Hey, Dave, you still beating your wife?"

Having beer at all made you guilty of something, in my mind. Why have it then? Root beer tasted good and was satisfying.

"So, I can't have this, is what you're saying?" he asked midpour.

No, you cannot. Francis says never to drink. It's bad.

He went along with it to shut me up, but I know he had to have been thinking, "Jeez, isn't she supposed to be in acting school? What kinda place is it again?" and bracing himself for the day I started wearing Holy Undergarments and eventually announced I was moving to Utah with a suspendered guy named Elijah who saw the world the way I did and if they loved me, they would please respect my decision.

A few days later, I was sitting in history class when I was called into the office. I had an important phone call.

"Hello, dahhhhrrrrrrlinnkkkk."

I don't even know how he knew what school I went to.

Francis was inviting me to accompany him to the Pantages Theater that night to see Sandy Duncan in *Peter Pan*. He wanted to expose me to the theater. It was verified: I indeed had the power to control things with my thoughts.

Francis called me at school!

Francis called me at school!

Francis called me at school!

Francis called me at school!

Francis called me at school!

I'd wear the camel-hair knickers with the Victorian top, or should I wear the island-flower purple and red that I made in Sewing with the fluttery white crepe top with the solitary diagonal ruffle?

There was so much to be done before a girl could be ready to go one-on-one with her octogenarian acting teacher. And I still had to get through one miserable period (P.E., of course) before I could go home.

Would we go in a limousine?

"Ahhhhhhhh! Right in the nuts!" Tina Chastain grunted gleefully when a softball hit a fellow student. I was sitting on a bench at the far side of the field, still nursing that groin pull, and I looked up from the *Playbill* I had tucked into a science book. Tina was the only girl I've ever heard use that word "nuts," and even though she was a coarse hillbilly, and practically a boy herself, it just didn't sit well with me. I didn't like that term "nuts."

She turned her curly head in my direction, but I quickly looked only slightly away, as if I had been watching the softball practice.

There was no shortage of girls upon whom Tina could've hung her rage. Far, far, dorkier girls than I. There was a girl I'd seen in the halls who looked just like a rat with a mustache. I was not particularly noteworthy; like I said, just a year before I had been an occasionally admired, well-socialized preteen. There must've been something about me that got through to her—something that jumped right off the page and grabbed her. To Tina Chastain, at least, I popped.

My *Playbill* was ripped from my hands and I jumped. Tina was behind me.

" 'Bob Fosser's Dancin'?' What is this fucking dirt shit? Did Pa—"

And that was all I really heard. I saw her mouth slit was twisting, which meant she was talking, and she wasn't calling me a goose, I knew that much.

"Wow," I thought, "this is a terrible situation. I must try to recapture this feeling when I'm playing Rosalie in *The Children's Hour.*"

And then my neck was in the crook of her arm and she was squeezing.

The feeling of the front of your neck meeting the back of your neck is stunning. It feels rough, and you suddenly become aware of the space that was there and now isn't. You think to yourself, "I didn't know this part could go back that far. No one's ever done this to me. This is really odd. The throat is so much like a rubber tube, like a hose. Like a hollow eel."

And now I needed to breathe but I could not.

And I saw myself with a French braid running down my back, wearing that cherry red rayon skirt that I had made in Sewing last summer—the one with the big purple island flower—and I was gliding the hall of my new school. This was the vision I'd had in my head when I told my mom that I wanted to be someone the other kids admired. I was pausing to offer guidance tempered with camaraderie to a fellow student who had lost her way. Mom, I said, I just want to be someone they look to. I want them to know me.

And again I needed to breathe but really could not. My head is . . . head, not . . . good. Not good, head. Vicky Goodhead. Give good head.

Ohhhhhhhhhhhh.

And then Tina let me go; just dropped me like a fickle hawk, emotionless as the Manchurian Candidate. She wandered away and left me with my life, but also with the awkward job of facing those few kids who had just seen me being choked. What is the dignified thing to do in this case? Besides the coughing and neck grabbing, which is involuntary? Does anyone know? Do you say anything? Do you give a little après-choke shrug and carry on with what you were just doing? I don't remember how I dealt with it.

Oh yes, I took massive amounts of drugs. Just remembered.

After much tribulation, I settled on the camel knickers and the Victorian top.

Mom and Dad drove me to the Academy, even more excited for my *Peter Pan* date with Francis than I was.

"He must really think you're talented!" said my Midwestern dad.

"Gee, you're not kiddin'!" echoed my Midwestern mom. Until I spent time around other kids, my parents had me saying things like "I'll have a can of pop" and "Let's go to the show."

Besides the fulfillment of the Francis fantasy, it had been rather a shitty day. Before the choking, even, lunch with Vicky had been strained. All I had said was, "So, there was a pretty funny *Benson* on last night," and she gave me back nothing, again. She couldn't even manage her one-word answers anymore. I had no choice but to fill in the gaps. " 'Gee, Stacey,' " I said, " 'I missed it. What happened on the episode?' " And she got all huffy at me. "Well, you sit there, every day, and you don't say a goddamn word" was all I said before she told me she didn't have to take this, grabbed her lunch bag, grabbed her book bag, and stood. As she walked away, I heard her make a snide comment. Something about working the wrong muscles.

Everything was better inside the Pantages Theater in Hollywood. While waiting for the show to start, Francis and I continued the conversation we hadn't been having in the car on the ride over. I pretended to ponder the ceiling before saying, calculatedly, that it reminded me of the Sistine Chapel in Rome, which it looked nothing like. Subtle, kid, real subtle.

At that, Francis's eyes flared with Czechoslovakian heat. "Ohhhh, dahhhhharrrlink." He smiled. "You have been to Italy?"

Yeah, man. I'd been all over Italy: Rome, Florence, Venice, Pompeii. I wasn't some skanky North of the Boulevard public school kid. My mother didn't use Aqua Net or say "fuck." We didn't own Jet Skis or drink diet drinks. My brother worked at Pep Boys and was going to be a photojournalist, okay? My dad had a powder blue vinyl jacket, sure, but he was still a decent man. I may not have been in a Devo video like Mona, but I had ducked my head to float into watery caves in Capri, where the water is so *absolutely teal*. You simply have to see it, but you won't, you Millikan Junior High assholes. I had an agent, and a headshot, and I was sitting here, in knickers, being exposed to the theater by Francis Lederer. Sandy Duncan sings, "I'm flying, I'm flying!" and I'm flying with her. Look at me, Nancy and Cathy! You, too, Goodhead. Choke on it, Tina Chastain. I'm flying over the whole world, and telling all of you who I am. And if I ever see Michael Keaton again, I'm going to tell him, too.

Francis wanted to know more about my travels as we walked down Hollywood Boulevard after the show. I told him that my dad was the art director for a big travel company, and because of that, we got free airfare anywhere in the world, as long as we took the same flight as one of their assembled tours. He was impressed. He asked me the name of the company, and the strangest thing happened.

We were just in front of Dos Burritos, the little burrito shack where, years and years from then, I'd so often sit, undershowered, unshaven, eating what's called a soft tostada, my only meal that week, and trying to figure out the easiest way to get over to the Chateau Marmont Hotel, where the singer Evan Dando would certainly give me free drugs. I looked down just then, and at my feet was a Unitours brochure—one that my dad had designed! What did it mean? Francis laughed. It certainly was odd. I think it meant that tonight was the Night of My Life of 1983, that magic was in the air, blowing exotic brochures at my feet. I didn't know yet all the sadness I'd someday feel at this spot. It didn't matter, because tonight, anything was possible. Tonight, the whole world was my soft tostada.

I want to say that at the end of the evening, we sat in Francis's Cadillac in the Academy alley, and he made me explain to him every little thing I enjoyed about the night's performance and then gave me a lecture about how shows like *Peter Pan* weren't really free, and that he hoped he could count on me to remember the sacrifice he had made for my benefit, and that in the future, he would remind me of this night, and I would get an opportunity to show that I was grateful, but not tonight, because my parents were going to be there soon. But that's not what happened. I think he just dropped me off and I said thank you, and my mom and dad said thank you, and we all drove to our homes.

And not long after, my headshot was on the wall of stars, where it might even remain to this day. The American National Academy of Performing Arts was a part of me, and now I was a part of it. My goofily smiling head, my shameful brows, and the Many Moods of Me on the other side could now begin their slow, mellow descent into the plaster wall.

We all want to wipe the place from our memories, but that (as you know, Ms. Hunt) is impossible. Cheese Nips stain, and no matter how well you may admonish and plead, "Out, out, damn Nip," and in what kind of accent, that orange dust remains like gunshot residue.

People came and went at the Academy. People like that Sleazy Angie with the synthetic Malibu Barbie hair that her mother bleached at home, and the teenage boy ballet teacher who, while crouching down to give me routine correction, unfolded my pink-slippered foot into the blue Spandex pillow of his crotch, an occurrence that still produces a phantom feeling atop my toes from time to time.

My agent Lee sent me on lots of auditions, but not a lot was happening. I didn't even get one callback from an open call for a role in *Six Weeks* with Dudley Moore, I lost out on the role of Young Meg in *The Thorn Birds* to whom? Sydney Penny, of course, and commercials were a wash. I wasn't popping.

Then, at thirteen and a half, I landed a role on a show called *Crisis Counselor* for my ability to cry on cue. I was the goody-goody younger sister of a delinquent played to perfection by none other than Sleazy Angie. The show was a real therapy session of a fake family by a real counselor and it was all improvised based on extensive fictional background information. How about that, Larry David?

Suddenly, I was taken to a bigger agency to meet a new agent, who had the advantage of not having met us in the park. He told my mother and father all the big plans he had for me and asked, Was I ready? Was I one of those tough-skinned kids who could deal with the pressure?

Of course not, but my oldest sister, Lee (not my agent Lee), was astonished when she saw me at my parents' friends' party. She hadn't seen me in a few weeks, since *Crisis Counselor,* and she claims I shook her off. That I flipped my hair and spoke of agents and auditions, and bragged about hanging around the set of *Silver Spoons* with my friend Julie, who was friends with Ricky Schroder. She said I was turning into someone she didn't know, and that the sluttish image of me that day bothered her for several years afterward.

But my sister is mostly full of shit. I doubt I was that bad. I may have trotted out somewhat of an arrogant air, it was the Sobels' annual High Holiday Party after all, but I'm sure I didn't flip hair and say anything too outlandish. I know I didn't sample the thumbprint cookies and pronounce them "unremarkable" or "not as good as cocaine, which I get for free from my new Hollywood contacts," and I am absolutely certain I did not emerge from the pool changing room, red lipstick smeared around my lips, skirt hiked, and proceed to grind my crotch into the gabardined knees of the middle-aged men while asking, "You want fucky-fucky my mouth, American Joe?" I *know* I didn't do that.

School got better. Vicky perked back up to one-word responses, and eventually landed a bag-girl job at Vons supermarket, which she seemed to really like—probably because her name tag just said "Vicky." Tina was gone, off on one of her Woody Guthrie–like rambles again. Maybe she was living out of a Jantzen book bag on Hollywood Boulevard, or maybe she was jumpin' trains and doin' odd jobs for Dep money. I imagine she eventually got herself together and landed a job at a poultry processing plant, where she is to this day forming the strips America loves.

One evening, between Acting and Jazz, I stopped by the office to get a script from Dorothy's filing cabinet. I was finally ready to attempt *The Women,* and even though I knew every scene by heart by that point, it was always exciting to hold the actual papers in my hand. I was getting to see what the older girls saw, and read what they read, and I couldn't wait to get up onstage next week and perform what I'd been seeing for so many years, with the same inflections. Dorothy riffled through the cabinet, spouting her paranoia about people stealing things, using them and not returning them, when my eyes drifted down to the desk at my right. It was a photo of Dorothy and Joan Crawford standing outside some movie premiere or other, one I'd glanced at many times, but now I noticed something odd. Dorothy, with her arms hidden in a muff, seemed to be levitating a little above the sidewalk, like a genie flying in to cackle and scold someone. And the edges around her looked weird, kind of white, like the edges of a photograph but not quite the same photograph, but perhaps one that had been cut up and affixed—

"Here it is," she said, handing me the mimeographed scene and making me promise again that Mr. Lederer said I was allowed to learn it.

Poor Dorothy. Poor Joan. Poor Dorothy and no Joan. Poor Dorothy, going upstairs to her bows, and her old lipsticks, and more of her Missy s, where I supposed she'd sit and stare at whispery, blue-hued paintings of ballerinas and gray poodles until it was time to come down and teach Speech. Poor Joan Crawford, holding up her house like some misguided Greek goddess, scooting across her great empty floor at something always just out of reach. Right cheek, left cheek, right cheek, left cheek, learning a new word a day, and not putting red food next to yellow food. Ass by ass. "And look!" she's thinking, "I'm also cleaning the floor! Isn't that something? Oh, Mamacita missed a spot over there, and over there. Must leave her a note. Also must remind her to stuff my Chanel suit sleeves with less 'avarice.' Right, left, reach! Reach! See, I can be this, or this, or this, I pop! Do you want me to pull taffy? I can do it! Look at these arms, these are taffy-pulling arms!" She's donning a top hat, tucking a cane underarm, and descending down the stairs. "Avarice! (and kick!) Avarice! (and kick!). Use it in a sentence! Watch me pop! This is MY WAY OF LIFE. THIS IS MY WAY OF LIFE. AND STEP AND KICK AND STEP AND KICK!"

* * *

Today's Hollywood is basically bereft of Pioneer Chickens, which is good, and Colonel Sanders is dead, thank God. I saw a portrait of his widow once. She was wearing a sunny yellow dress, and the sun gleamed in her stiff gold hair. She was shot from behind as she surveyed the massive classical lawn at the Sanderses' Kentucky Palace. I felt like she didn't want her face shown, that the most she could do was stare at vague points on the lawn where, who knows, chickens of every natural color with dappled plumes of black and copper and orange and gray might've liked to scratch and peck the day long. That for now, the lawn was beautiful and green, but that any minute it would run red with blood.

They've since cleared away most of the runaways from Hollywood Boulevard and replaced them with a big, big mall and cheery-cheeked tourists in low-rise pants and platform thongs that wander hither and thither. But the little Dos Burritos stand remains, and people say a ghost haunts its cramped and grimy space—a child, an angelic little child, with stiff golden locks and the sad, lipless frown of Phil Collins. They say, late at night, you can see her with her hammy arms extended, and that every so often, people will start to cough for no reason at all.

And I sit at auditions, with all the too new girls with enviable noses who don't know the first thing about Claudette Colbert, speaking the speech as I've pronounced it to you, who've never worn camel knickers, or had bad eyebrows, or felt the feeling of a collapsed neck. But I suppose they all have their own stories.

I left the Academy when I realized that I preferred to

hang out in torn stockings with kids with dyed hair and offensive T-shirts. Dorothy sighed and said that I "just didn't want it badly enough." As if anyone can ever really know what anyone else wants badly.

I can still tap-dance quite well and I don't cause too many problems.

Love me?

SUNSETS

I'm going back over the hill, again, all dressed in black. A concho belt's graceful leather tassels swing low, brushing the thigh tops, and from my neck hangs a pendant of the finest sidewalk vendor onyx. On one wrist, a leather-and-concho bracelet; on the other, a trapezoid of pony fur, black and white, somewhat matted. A tiny silver ring in the shape of an ankh completes my pinkie. This is not how I envisioned it, yet this is how it is.

Missy Nacht, my best casual friend, fresh out of her scoliosis back brace and ready to do the town, sits in the passenger seat of the silver Celica (my mother's). She wears her newly dyed black hair in a chin-length bob, which has blunt ends, all the way around. This is the telltale shape that keeps her tethered to 1982, bodily, spiritually. She is dressed partially in black. We drive through the canyon to a club called the Whisky a Go Go on Sunset Boulevard. It's a trip we make often these days and nights. Missy stares ahead, untroubled, chattering away about boys, and funny sounds that cars make. I listen just enough.

It has been three years since *Annie* and I am quite a different person. About twelve hundred suns have set since I first stood, afraid, on Sunset Boulevard.

That was '82. The movie version of the Broadway musical *Annie* had just opened. Cathy, Mona, Christine, Julie, all of my performing arts friends, and I had been following this thing very closely. It had been the talk of the whole previous year: the nationwide search for the ideal Annie. Who was the One who could blow everyone away with her gumption? And her zing? The One who could ball up her little orphan fist and say "Leapin' Lizards!" and really make you believe it?

I didn't try out, of course. I was too old and decrepit to play Annie. Plus, I never could shake the feeling that there was something wrong with singing that "Tomorrow" song. It seemed to bother people. People thought differently of little girls who went around singing "Tomorrow."

They finally found their Annie, I believe, soot-covered and living in a locker in a train station with a suitcase full of performing fleas and nothing to eat but a hard, crusty roll. Her name was Aileen Quinn. "Ayyyyyyleen, not Eileen, Ayyyyyyleeen," Cathy corrected me.

But no matter, soon the whole world would know to say "Ayyyyleeeeen." "Eileen" would become a secondary name. Now that Aileen Quinn was to be Annie, I remember telling myself, she'd have the rest of her life served to her on a *plate*.

We all went over the hill to see it on opening day at the

Chinese Theatre in Hollywood, which cost us each five dollars. *Five dollars.* For a *matinee even.* Movies were now five dollars, and there would never again come a time when movies would be less.

Aileen's tight red curls and big face freckled up the screen, like we all knew it would. Yet she never worked again.

Afterward, we wandered freely around Hollywood on our own as big kids would. We found ourselves on Sunset, face-to-face with a boarded-up building where punk had recently been.

"It was called the Whisky," Cathy said, in her prim, scolding way. Cathy was the elder of our group, so the onus of fear projection was on her. The place was closed down, she told us, because of all the violence that was caused there. There were nightly cheek stabbings with safety pins, reservoirs of spit and unhygienic doings at every turn. They might just decide to vomit on you if they didn't like you.

I'd seen a TV show or two on punk. One had a girl pierce her cheek with a safety pin right on camera. And the newsmagazine series *Eye on L.A.* did a segment on punky fashion. Connie Chung went to a punk boutique that sold a one-of-a-kind jacket that was made exclusively of shellacked cockroaches. I'd also seen an interview with a mean, mean lady with a Mohawk called Wendy O. Williams. Everyone was leery of her because she wore only electrical tape on her breasts and carried a chain saw. I remember the precise warning she gave: "Rock and roll is not your friend," she said. "Rock and roll *will* bite your face off," she said, stressing the *"will."*

There were still flyers and graffiti on the outside of the Whisky: "Fuck!" most of it said. There was a lot written about who currently ran the fuck and who had been previously running the fuck. The Nunz was a band name I recognized. They went for a nun-thing, and there was the famous Whisky a Go Go go-go girl mascot dancing through all the chaos even though she hardly belonged anymore.

This was a wicked place. It was very plainly wagging its tongue toward me and going, "Wooooo. Woo, wooo! I'll get you!"

I fingered the remains, until Cathy told me not to. I could get dried cheek blood or saliva on my finger, which could get infected if I had a cut and that person had had something, which they probably did.

But that was '82. Now I'm here, with Missy, trying to make the current scene, which, to my delight, is said to have come to 1985 by way of glam rock, my beloved. The current semblance, however, which has just started to bloom on the Sunset Strip (the one that is sprouting black fingernails through the cracks in the concrete and scratching people very rudely on the ankles), has been unfortunately degraded these last few years by some heavy metal achenes, their fluffy filaments carried on the unpredictable winds. (Some of which were of the mutant albino leather jacket strain, they say.) These seeds mingled with the late-seventies-punk topsoil and bore a hybrid that is something like late-early Aerosmith. It's hearty and seems frost-resistant, but lacks something, I don't know. I know it's not real glam, but I'll take what I can get. This is how I have to explain things to Missy. I don't think she really understands, but Missy tries. She does. She puts on a suitable outfit and sits up straight, repeating her little phrases.

I'd been crying out for glam since I first held the paper sleeve of my sister's Ziggy Stardust record and ogled the beautiful smooth moon man in the quilted moon suit who regarded me with clear eyes and sang to me of milkshakes, the world's end in five years (five, my age, a wondrous number to me), Vaseline, and a host of other things I could relate to.

Then, 'long about my twelfth year, my resting, bashful crush resurfaced and caught like glamorous fire. I ravished every Bowie thing I could find.

Concurrently, my brother grew a mustache and moved to San Diego, leaving behind a beige bedroom that I promptly turned into the California Institute for the Advancement of David Bowie Studies. I worked very diligently, day and night. "Dave" became family. My parents, seated by themselves over their grapefruit halves, would sigh and say, "She's in her Dave room, reading her Dave books, singing her Dave songs, thinking her Dave thoughts." Often I took dinner on a tray.

I expanded; I looked into what David's friends and influencers had been up to. I came across his seething little buddy Iggy Pop and enjoyed him. I got unhealthily close to Roxy Music, and to the others.

So I am quixotic about this new scene, this mid-eighties cluster of what people will eventually call "Sunset Strip Hair Bands." But I never got to have the real thing. I never got to wake up in some hotel somewhere with the New York Dolls strewn about me. The closest I'd ever gotten to David Bowie was the hyper-lifelike poster (*Lodger* period, where he's wearing the red blazer and has his natural hair color—my preference) on the main wall of the California Institute that followed me around with its eyes, especially in the beige half-light. He could see me, too, and indicated that as best he could with little winks and nods, but it wasn't the same. And the closest I got to Bryan Ferry was when I looked at the poster of the Eiffel Tower at sunset on the wall of my bedroom and pretended it was the view from our hotel in Paris. Paris was our getaway, our "place," we called it. We'd go there on a whim. (With Bryan and me, everything was on a whim. Whims were all we had.) Each time, we'd find it just as we left it. So, so sweet. The tinkling piano in the next apartment the only sound. The only light, the twilight from that frozen sunset that I have spoken of. We'd eat languidly, unctuous custards on small plates, and do things to each other with our mouths. Then we'd go for a stroll in the perdurable coral-colored sunset, which was never ending or beginning. We'd stop somewhere for profiteroles and I'd ask him if a never-ending sunset could perhaps be a sun*rise*? "Is that birdsong? Or the calling of the nightingale?" we'd ask each other, only half seriously. "Ahhh, *qui sait?*"

Not I, for it is 1985 and I am sixteen and I want to go out, and these Sunset Strip bands are the hard Fig Newtons from the back of the cupboard: they'll do.

Once again, Missy is brooding over the shortness and sameness of her hair. She wants it to be like mine, copious and luxuriant with little torrents of gold and copper through-out. The kind of hair you could modestly gather around yourself when you drift off in a hotel somewhere with the New York Dolls. I don't want her to feel bad. "At least it's black," I console her. "I'll never get to have black hair, my mother would kill me." But not Missy's mother, a deeply religious depressive with a foreign name who doesn't care what Missy does to her hair or face or body. The black was my idea. Not only did I think it would bode well for us on the scene, but I couldn't take the shade she'd been dyeing it all year: Wella Color Charm "Cyclamen." It was the color of a redwood picnic table abandoned to the elements, but she admired it so. She thought the sun ignited the suggestion of purple. "It's so pretty. Isn't it so pretty?" I'd have to say it was so pretty or listen to her cry and cry all day long like a little baby. Now it's #51 Black, and #51 Black it will stay.

Winding, winding, winding, we two daughters of the Valley wind through the canyon, which spits our Celica out onto the Sunset Strip. We continue to the reopened Whisky, to see a show by a band called, simply, China.

From my observation tower in 2007, I will see crowds gathered in front on softly sloping sidewalks, dappled with the emollients of so much rock history and so many pieces of old gum and other protein splatters ground into the concrete by heavy cowboy heels. (I will feel the weight of the cowboy heels.) Five or so feet above, I will see hanging a layer of puffy dyed black hair, puffy bleached blond hair, and just there, the small glint of a sparkly scarf tossed over the shoulder of a laughing young man.

*   *   *

Missy and I have been to a few of these Sunset Strip shows already; we'd seen China the night before last, Damn Yankees a few times, Jetboy once, Faster Pussycat, and some band called the Children's Hour from San Diego that doesn't count and was Missy's idea. The one capable band in this current cluster, the only one that gives off any starlight at all, is Guns N' Roses. Guns N' Roses has just advanced past the small clubs to the next tier. And probably because of this, people at these shows speak a good deal of shit about them. Guns N' Roses' integrity has been called into question. It is not advisable to like them.

I'm beginning to recognize some faces, some scarves. The same people come to all these things. There are certain ones, however, who look to have come up from different seeds—the conifers of highlighted curls and bronzed faces interspersed in the crowd indicated other roots (variations of the Whitesnake plant, the Bon Jovi fern). Inwardly, these strains made me doubt my judgment. They are perennials, I must tell myself. They come with the terrain. There will always be, I tell myself, a guy in a cropped white leather jacket somewhere nearby. He's there whether you see him or not—with his girlfriend in frosty lipstick—and I shouldn't let it hamper my good time. It's not as if I will become infected by certain elements around me, will I? Will I one day discover myself, someone's black-T-shirted common-law wife, in a small apartment administering his perm, the chemicals singeing my fingertips, and wonder just what became of me?

Missy doesn't think about things as hard as I do. She has no glam agenda. Or any allegiance to anything I can decipher. I know she wants a car, and longer hair, but in all the time we've been best friends (two years and eight months), she has never demonstrated a preference for a band or even a style of music. Although classified, mainly by blood (she is the younger sister of acclaimed local punk Matt Nacht), as a member in good standing of what the San Fernando Valley deems "punk" during the early mid-eighties, I never see her take it upon herself to seek out musical offerings of any kind, unless you count the Children's Hour, which I don't. We share an obsession with the Cult, whose Hollywood Palladium show on the She Sells Sanctuary tour is an event so holy to us that we use it to mark time, but I always suspect her adoration stems more from Ian Astbury's scarves than anything else. She'll garnish her written correspondence with requisite acknowledgments to certain bands: the Cure, Siouxsie, the Cult, all rendered correctly (the big *i,* little *o,* etc.). When pressed, she has a casual knowledge of Black Flag, but for all I know, Missy goes home and listens to Howard Jones every night.

With her blunt ends.

I find myself missing dear Melanie Tsongus quite often. She was Greek, and lived near the IHOP, but she understood glam. We were friends in the summer of 1983 until destiny took us to different schools. She was new at it, very new, but she was malleable. When we met, all she owned was *ChangesOneBowie* and *Let's Dance,* but with my help she began to explore some others. The last thing I remember was her tan hands cracking the shrink-wrap on *The Man Who Sold the World.* She was willing. She had the will. Her father, the bearded and strict Phoebus Tsongus, was nice enough to drive us to Anaheim Stadium to see Dave on the Serious Moonlight tour. Her little brother came along and covered his ears. That was August, and summer soon ended. Later, with the release of David's next record, *Tonight,* and the heartbreak of its single, "Blue Jean," I looked to Melanie to commiserate, but I never found her again.

I thought I saw her in a crowd near the stage during the Glass Spider tour, but it could've just been some other Greek face in the darkness.

So Missy is all I have. Many people think that I only sought out and manipulated a friendship with her because I was in love with Matt, which I did, because it was true. But since then, I've built up a real tolerance for the old girl, even laugh sometimes at her impression of an old car horn (*a—oooo-ga, a—oooo-ga*), and it's not like we don't have fun times. We do. Like when we call the "hotlines" listed on some of the band's flyers.

One afternoon in my room, we hunched over the receiver as she dialed the hotline for China, whose flyer we had been handed outside the Whisky.

"Um, hi, is this someone in China?" [Giggle, giggle.]

"Yeah, dude," said a male voice.

"Is this the singer?" [Giggle, giggle, giggle.]

"Yeah, this is. Who's this?"

"This is, um [giggle] Samantha and [silence, receiver cupping, questions] Anastasia." [Back slaps, stifled laughter.]

"Rad. You ladies like to party?"

"We might. We wanna come to your show. Which one are you?" [Grabbing of flyer, studying of photograph.]

"What?"

"On the flyer?"

"Oh, I'm in the middle with the zebra belt."

[Clutching of hands, excitement.]

"Oh, you're the hot one!"

"Fuck yeah. Where are you guys?"

"Oh, we live in Malibu. My brother's a director."
[Uncontrollable laughter.]

"That's cool. The beach is rad."

"Yeah, it is. What's your name?"

"Clark."

"Oh, hey, Clark."

"Hey."

And it went on like this for several afternoons. When it became obvious that Missy and I weren't two eighteen-year-old-model half sisters whose brother was director of *Beverly Hills Cop* and that we didn't live in his Malibu beach house while he was away making a movie in France, and that we didn't have any weed, and we weren't actually going to come over and double-team him any night that week, Clark China (it was customary for many band members upon joining or forming a band to take on the band name as one's surname: Axl Rose, Tracii Guns, Clark China, Ted Yankee, Stan Poison, etc.) grew tired of our little game.

She always took it too far. I could've talked glam with him. That would have certainly set me apart from the other tarts calling the China hotline.

Most girls around these places at this time doing those things with those kinds of guys are named Traci Black, or

Lisa Black, or Michelle Black, and are either strippers or prospective strippers who live with their divorced dads, who don't care what they do. The Tracis and Lisas (or the Michelles) have their own apartments, Ford Fieros, blow, and can buy Jack Daniel's for the men they love. Missy and I know some of these girls peripherally; some of them are colleagues of girls we know or have heard of who have been banished to Jack London, the little continuation school at the far, far edge of our campus (beyond the parking lot). Some years later, certain ones turned up all loosey-goosey in hot tubs in the movie *Decline of Western Civilization Part II: The Metal Years.*

But there is as yet no hot tub for me, the deserving one who's passed so many close nights in her yellow room with her records when no one came. Alone, me. Staring through my Paris "window," my Bowie sailor hat pushed back on my head. All the painstaking research, all the attention to detail, all those lonely hours logged at turntable, at book, at liner note and sleeve, the small and rhythmic bows I made, surely they must be worth something to someone.

Maybe to Taime Downe?

He is the cottony-blond lead singer of Faster Pussycat who works at Retail Slut on Melrose during the day, just until his band starts to take off. But no matter, someone in an elite Melrose retail position such as that enjoys nearly all the prestige one does when in a band, at least in my eyes. I buy most everything I own at Retail Slut, sometimes from him when he's there, straight from his densely ringed fingers. And all those head scarves. And all that onyx, oh! Somewhere in the world there had to be an onyx drought.

Faster Pussycat is the band for which I have the fondest feelings. Musically, they are not better or worse than any others, but I like their name, and they emit a sort of rarefied vibe that gets through to me somehow. I think it harks back to the impression I once got from a young Hanoi Rocks, although probably in hair and scarves only. Faster Pussycat songs are not good songs. I can recognize just one from the shows I've been to. It's about having just gotten back from the "best whorehouse in town." Missy pines for Brent Muscat, Faster Pussycat's fawnlike, onyx-haired guitar player, who seems affable enough. There's also a guy whose name I don't know whose stare, in the flyer picture, smolders with the intensity of an entire pack of wolves, cooked down into one expression. And there are a couple of others, and then there is the Man of Onyx.

I don't understand his name. Taime Downe? Is it meant as a play on "tie me"? And if so, why would that need a play? Just call yourself "Tie Me Down." "Tymie" if you like. There are no rules. Or why not "T'aime Pussycat"? As in the French, "love you," and then the "pussy" part? But who can say? Maybe it's just his real name.

Missy and I had been to Retail Slut a couple of days earlier to buy the tickets for last night's show (you could buy your tickets directly from Taime at the store). While he readied them, I noticed a professional-quality photo of a girl on the wall behind the register, and it was signed to him with lip prints. It said her name was Tracy Black. She had the same spun-sugar hair, white skin, amber eyes, as he. I had seen her before: last summer, waiting in line at the Hollywood Palladium for the Siouxsie show. (Missy's idea, not mine—hard as I tried, I couldn't get into Siouxsie. I hated the way she drew her eyeliner downward. How could one justify such an abnormal, unflattering artifice? Eyes go up, not down. Pretty eyes go *up*.) She sat primly on the ground in her leopard coat all day and I watched her continually daub herself with Coty loose powder and stare into her wire stand-up mirror while talking all kinds of lofty shit about all the bands she was friends with, personally. She was exactly the kind of asshole I knew I could be, with just a few adjustments. The following day, I went to the drugstore and bought the little hatbox of Coty powder with the gold and cottony puff design, and a metal wire-legged mirror.

Taime gave us our tickets but wasn't very polite to us. He practically threw them at us, practically flung them from his dung-beetle-black fingernails, shiny and chipped. Then Missy, a terrible decoder of human subtleties, told Taime that I also wanted to buy the hat.

"She wants to get the hat."

"What?"

"The red one. The red bolero hat. She wants it. Can she try it on, please?"

"No, I don't," I jump in. "I don't want the hat," I say, and steer her out of the store.

The Celica ride back over the hill was tense. Missy couldn't understand that just because I may have said something in passing, all last week, about wanting the hat and how cool I thought the hat was and that I was planning on getting it that day, that she should leave these things up to me.

Still, we went to the show that night and stood as close

as we could get—right under Taime the whole time. He sang the song about the best whorehouse and everyone went crazy, grabbing for him and sometimes catching hold of the scarves he tied to his mike stand.

But tonight it is China again. I don't care too much about it; my illusions about Clark China were dashed when I first saw him in person and noticed he was stoutly haunched, but Missy is still devoted and harbors hope of something blooming there, although they've never met and the hotline number has been disconnected. That is why she is wearing a good deal of white tonight. At the end of the last show, Clark had posed a challenge to the audience: "At the next show," he said, "I want to find my Angel in White." He had given us an assignment, essentially. "Who will be my Angel in White?" he asked the crowd about three times.

Of course, Missy wants to be the Angel in White, but she is understandably unsure, so she wears mostly white, but with a black skirt. She can always play it off like she's come straight from a catering job, if it ever comes to that.

I move around the club, my aura a little gray oval, creeping into the gaps left by the flow of rowdy rockers, who all know each other. I'm tiny, hesitant, stupid. I'm just a trusting Valley girl, the result of thousands of years and thousands of intertwined varietals of Central Asia peasant, and I've ended up here, in conch belt and bolo tie, hoping to order a 7 Up from the bartender, who just looks past me.

Then comes the flood of shameful thoughts that unleash themselves when I feel the ghastly maw of rock readying itself on my face. The feeling I used to get when I sat in the lunchroom and unwrapped a sandwich from home, the feeling of writing the name of a band I loved on my book cover, and then covering it up once at school. They always come at the worst times, these shameful thoughts: I am in high school and I enjoy art history / I think it's fun to sip Nestea on a summer night while watching the Dodgers with Mom and Dad / I confuse "blow job" and "snow job" / I like washing the dog with my dad on the weekends. It's fun, we put Sandy in the big green wheelbarrow and when we're done he goes, shake shake shake, and gets us all wet! And, on New Year's Eve, my sister makes really good chocolate fondue and we watch the ball drop. Her boyfriend directed a documentary about a guy named Jim Dunn who raced funny cars. It was called *Funny Car Summer.* We all have *Funny Car Summer* T-shirts, *Funny Car Summer* T-shirts, *Funny Car Summer* T-shirts. . . .

I now am so ashamed I even *considered* buying the red felt bolero hat. How dare I think of myself at that level? The time will come, I hope, when I will breeze into the Whisky or the Roxy or the Troubadour on the arm of some Rikkii Yankee or Clark China or Leon Guns or Stan Poison, and peek out like a foggy-eyed sex doe from the brim of the red bolero hat, and not have to say much. People will think, "Here they are, the king and queen of the Sunset Strip!" Some bandmate of his, for all are like big brothers to me (how they coddle me!), will turn from the bar with a White Russian for me, or a brandy Alexander. Perhaps I will at that point have even started to go by the name Brandi Alexander. People will say, "Look at them! They rise at sundown and begin their waltz of decadence, those two." And they'll be right.

I get my 7 Up, and Missy and I stand by the stage. A girl from Jack London, Michelle, who knows someone who knows Muscat, comes up. She says that the girl (Traci?) said that Taime was really mad.

Really mad?

Last night at the show, she said, some girl was grabbing his crotch the whole time and he couldn't concentrate and she said he said he thought it was me!

"Me? It wasn't me!"

A girl dressed head to toe in white lace walks by. She has a perm.

"Well, he thinks it was you, he said it was that little girl who was standing right under him, who comes in the store all the time with her friend."

But it wasn't me, it wasn't me. There were hands near me, doing that, but they weren't mine, but it wasn't me. It may have seemed like me, but it wasn't me. I would never do that. I would never, I would never, I would never!

My chest collapses into itself, leaving an indelible bolero-shaped hollow that will never go away.

Et tu, Taime?

In the mid-nineties, on Sunset, after the Lipliner Wars but before the Tooth-Whitening Revolution, it is the night of November 22. There is a party in honor of my birthday at my work, the Viper Room nightclub. In a photo, I am smiling unabashedly, and behind me members of the band Porno for Pyros chat blissfully, unaware they are in the picture. Moving out of frame is the actor Norman Reedus, who later becomes the face of Prada briefly. My dress is a black silk thing from a nauseatingly cliquish Sunset Boulevard boutique called Tracey Ross, where I get a discount. I drowsily extend my arm high in the air, because, as the club's booker, guest list controller, and personal friend of John Christopher Depp's, I have become the baroness of the Sunset Strip. No felt bolero for me. I'm wearing a tiara.

Due to a series of missteps, mis-sleeps, and rope-climbing burns, I have made it here, and I can talk all kinds of lofty shit about the bands I know personally. That cigarette burn in the backseat of my car? Dave Pirner from Soul Asylum did that. That is just one tiny, tiny example. I can get into any show, any party, any club without any preparation, and I can decide with just a flourish of ink who gets into mine. Aileen Quinn, Taime Downe, they won't ever get in.

I've let the sun set on my wrath so many times it's now a sunrise.

My day is something like this: I rise late, very late, and put on one of my many pairs of Daryl K jeans, which still hold the warm shape of my sexy thighs from the night before. My muscles are starting to atrophy, the doctor says, but I am so popular. Everyone wants to take me to lunch.

Entering the club, I see the killer that walks the street. Arthur "Killer" Kane, of the New York Dolls, walks right by the club every day around eleven. He lives nearby and is probably getting coffee or a paper. No one recognizes him, even though he looks the same. Every time I see him, I think, "There goes Killer Kane from the New York Dolls." And sometimes I think about how the club I work in, the Viper Room, used to be a club called Filthy McNasty's and it's in the background of the cover of the Sweet's album, *Desolation Boulevard,* but I can't think too long because I have to work.

I crawl into my little black velour office (the one that's known as "Johnny's private room," which he's been in about four times). Gift baskets and flowers and unsolicited band tapes clutter my area, which I toss aside. And the phone rings. It's been ringing all morning. For me, yes, for me.

I talk, drink coffee, growl, cackle, and smoke all day. I am instructed, when I am given this job, to study the business technique of Michael Corleone. I do. I'm that dumb.

'Long about 5 P.M., with no food to stave them off, a torrent of poisons careens into my skull, and I announce tearfully to the office staff that I am going next door for Twinkies. Back in my office, my black little pancreas of an office, I tear away the wrapper, eating my pastry with a rodent's trembling fingers, fitfully turning and gnawing, turning and gnawing. People leave me alone.

My job is to fill the club with at least three hundred drinking people each night except Tuesday, when it is the problem of another promoter. I have some help with Thursdays, too, because that is Martini Night, when everyone is supposed to pretend it's fun to pretend it's the forties. I've never had any yearnings like that. To me, these swing people are just nerds with unnecessarily ornate cigarette lighters. To persist with such a relic of a lighter takes heart, I guess, yet I have no respect for them. To be nostalgic for the handkerchiefs you've never carried takes something, I suppose, but nothing I want. And they have their own strange language. They speak in rhymin' riddles, or something. Sometimes, instead of talking, they just snap their fingers at each other, but it doesn't matter much if the other person gets it, it's usually just one swinger condoning another's hat. Lucky for me, the Thursday-night DJ books most of the swing bands.

But not every Thursday. Often it is my problem. Like now, I needed a headliner for the swing night. Who was it to be? I look through my Rolodex: Daddy Jump-Down? The Danglin' Dogs, the Shakin' Jakers? No good, they're out of town. The Rhymin' Riddles? (Did I invent them, or could I book them?)

And then there are a slew of bands with the word "rooster" in the title. They admired roosters, these swingers. And martinis. Martinis are the pinnacle. Swingers want to see everything in a martini glass. "Man, oh man," they think, "what if the whole world could be in a martini glass? Wouldn't that be slick? Wouldn't that be sharp? Wouldn't that be crackers, daddy-o?"

And why isn't anyone wearing black-and-white-striped pajamas with different-colored triangles sewn on the chest? That's very forties. How about dressing like a famished Red Army soldier? These people are cowards, frozen in mid–Lindy Hop with their bloomers exposed. They think they can tuck themselves into the folds of history and hide from rock and roll's scavenging teeth? These silly trends just anger rock. The jaws just get confused. They bite off a small piece and start to chew and then grow sad and stop. This club is so strange: one night it's this, one night it's that. And there goes Killer Kane! Why doesn't he ever even stop in?

The Razzle Cats? No, Jumpin' Jehoshaphats? Rattled Razzamatazzers, The Leapin' Lizards? No. The Swingin' Guys, the Hoppin' Johnnycakes, the Slam Bam Banana Jams? The Sultans of S-, Sultans of Sw-; the Rolodex card is faded. The Sultans of what? Swimming?

When people think about a nightclub, they think about sparkly scarves, primarily. What they don't know is that there are people who sit in black rooms without windows all day and make and take phone calls. They don't know how many times Harry Dean Stanton calls. They don't know what it's like to hide from Angela Bowie. They don't know the loneliness of a case of floppy disks that sits behind a desk on black carpet. They don't know the office manager will yell at you for spilling coffee on it, no matter how many rock stars you know. They don't know about the Twinkies.

In 2007, I will be quite sure that if a rat is prevented from gnawing on things, its front teeth will grow and grow until they slowly, oh so slowly, stab the animal in the neck, slowly, slowly killing it. I will have heard this somewhere. There's time for everything. Soon, maybe in three years, we will do away with time altogether. There will just be one huge honeycomb of incidents happening at once, and we will program in what order we want to experience it, even though there will not be any order either. If we miss something, we can always catch it again. Some people will put their time on "shuffle."

In 2007, I will find Taime's page on a popular social-networking Web site. Waggish Taime will list his age as "69." His occupation, "girl juice taster." He will be dressed in some black vinyl getup with not so subtle notes of the uniform of an SS officer, and his arm will be raised. He will foster such love for actor/comedian Denis Leary, he will find it necessary, under his "heroes," to list him twice. I will consider sending him a message to tell him that it was not I who grabbed him, that I only very gingerly, very meekly and respectfully, touched my index finger to the nib of his gray suede cowboy boot for a notch of a second because I was right there and it was right then and I knew the moment wouldn't come again, ever. And that's all I did. But I will decide not to, because my time will be more important than that. And besides, I only grazed the tip of his gray suede cowboy boot with the tiny tip of my finger, that's all.

I will think of Taime there, that hair, blond over white, in constant upheaval. He will certainly seek refuge from what are certainly grudges against Muscat, against the world, in his precious porn, and his favorite show, King of Queens. *I will see him there, lumpy leather couch, German cross on the wall, his face the stuff of rock and roll's cud: bloodless, pitted, having been chewed and rechewed these last twenty-four years. And laughing, either at* King of Queens, *or Denis Leary's* Rescue Me, *beer in hand. Just some intervals against the really big sunset. He'll hold up a withered, crooked finger and emit the one tiny final cry: "Pussy!" (He got to be a rock star for a couple of years once, but I'm sure it felt like a whole life.)*

I work at the Viper Room for a long time, and a lot of people come, but Dave never comes. Sue, the bar manager, dances away an entire night with someone who tells her he is Bryan Ferry, but who turns out to be an impostor.

Iggy comes, though. Iggy comes a lot, sometimes with a prostitute, and he becomes my little buddy. He calls out to me across a crowded room, and everyone turns to look at me.

He performs on our little stage, and I stand right up in the front. He does his whole thing, thrashing around like he does, flailing, bleeding, doing all the old stuff, and I think, "I'm liking this, I'm really liking this!" And, "I can't believe I'm getting to see this! This thing I like so much! What time is it? How long will this last? I could go for a milkshake after this. I wonder if I left the air-conditioning on in my apartment. I hope not, or it'll be freezing when I get home. Does everyone else think this is as great as I do? What a moment this is! Gee! I'm one of a select few who gets to see this. I wonder if this is the last song?"

MISS NOVEMBER

Once, I let a man named Richard take pictures of me naked.

It was 1989, when people in Los Angeles seemed to be putting away their Faith No More records and taking out their De La Soul records, and then throwing them both on the floor, unsure how to sort out all the feelings they were having, not just about slouchy white socks with black leather shoes, but about everything that was probably happening out there, in that place we called "the world." We had long since learned the proper way to mix wasabi into soy sauce, and I, like most of my generation, was wondering, What's next?

My best friend, Heidi, and I lived in a tidy apartment in the flats of Sherman Oaks, a few blocks from our childhood homes. Fresh out of high school, we bore the naive, peculiar sheen of people who have just realized they can eat what they like and stay up as late as they want. We kept up-to-date lists of the beverages we had on the refrigerator, hung Man Ray postcards on the walls, lounged on my parents' old gold couch, and slept soundly beneath brand-new black comforters. It was a dumb lifestyle, but it suited us fine. I commuted every day to the flat, dusty campus of California State University, Northridge, where I listened as young professors, with completely straight faces, defended the validity of Exene Cervenka as a poet and an artist, and Perry Farrell as an artistic poet, and both as valid poet-artists, who were still unwelcome in the canon of Dead White Men. I wore Crabtree & Evelyn rosewater lotion. I have never had a more blissful time. In photographs from the era, I smiled aloofly, and wore a wide, wide belt.

When I wasn't curled up with Alice Walker, or Zora Neale Hurston, I worked in an independent new and used record store on Melrose Avenue, which was still an important street on the map of explosive youth culture. Every store, except Privilege Shoes, meant something, and as an employee, you were like an agent of that culture peninsula, helping it explode. Our little yellow-and-purple-polka-dotted record store represented the grand artistic upheaval resulting from the switch from LP's to CD's, as well as a place where junkies could get sixteen dollars fast. Richard Fegley was often among the many solitary, determined-looking men who scoured the used bins on Saturday mornings and, hours later, arrived at the counter to pay for five 29-cent records with a hundred-dollar bill. I didn't know this denim-shirted guy with the cluster of white curls was a famous *Playboy* photographer, who had taken all kinds of shots of young Bebe Buell and Kim Basinger with their nudity draped over horses in the mist, on the beach. When he asked Todd, my boss, if I might be interested in doing a centerfold test, I didn't even look up from alphabetizing the cassingles.

"You'll never guess what my friend Richard just asked about Stacey," he said, lining his blazer pockets with cash from the register, as was his custom. Still reeling from the rush of the eighties and the radio promo job he snorted away, Todd loved to peel off a twenty and hand it to one of his many eager employees with instructions to "get us all some of that gelato crap, will ya?" He was the floppy-haired wizard behind the deal counter, twirling people's old John Fogerty and Average White Band records into store credit slips with the agility of Tom Cruise in *Cocktail*.

"I told him no, of course. Why?" he said, turning to me. "You don't want to do it, do you?"

Everyone had to fucking weigh in. My older sister cautioned me that I could not continue to be the person I was and also be a Playmate. "I'm almost positive you have to hang out at the mansion and do all that stuff and be involved," she said. Well, that was never going to happen. I wasn't much of an involver, nor could I see myself sitting demurely at the edge of the grotto in one of my vintage dresses, or wandering over to ask the DJ if he had any Camper Van Beethoven.

Heidi was more open to my role as photographic muse—I'd been the subject of her gothic-fantasy photo-essays since high school, particularly the Bustier and Blood series, where I am depicted, in lace bodysuit, gazing powerfully through a candelabra, or considering a novelty shrunken skull. She and I were no strangers to the magnitude of art photos. Our lives were art photos. Back then, in our little poolside apartment, nights were deep, warm pillowcases of dark, sexy promise, and each day bloomed anew with the chirping of birds and old Volkswagen engines.

The particulars of my test were handled by Stephanie Barnett at Playboy Enterprises, International. I was to report to the 9000 building on Sunset Boulevard—the one with the big bunny on top—at 8 A.M. Friday morning with my hair and face clean. I wondered, Were there girls in the world who actually needed to be told to show up for their nudie shots clean? I was from Sherman Oaks; no one needed to tell me to wash.

I was met by a petite blond makeup artist, I want to call her Pasha, in a breezy white outfit. I wouldn't say she liked me, but she was glad my skin wasn't "burnt to a crisp" like the others'. After she rolled my hair onto big electric rollers, she started my makeup, keeping everything quite peachy and tawny. Lost in the makeup room's wall-to-wall mirrors, she put as much makeup on herself as she did on me, and with the same applicators. But that wasn't the most distressing thing about her. The most distressing thing about her was that she was laboring under the impression that she had a long, secure, loving relationship with Mr. Don Henley. At one point during the day, "The Boys of Summer" came on the radio, and Pasha rolled her eyes. This happened to her all the time.

In between makeup and wardrobe, there was paper-work to be done, including the famous centerfold question-naire. I tried to emulate the full-bodied, girlie handwriting style I'd seen in the magazine, drawing out each *w* into a voluptuous ass, each lowercase *s* itself a generous teardrop of a breast, ready to ooze sweet cherry juice all over the reader. Turn-ons: Robert Rauschenberg, hardwood floors, Dolce & Gabbana, and sipping cappuccinos with friends. Someday, I hoped to meet the lead singer of Soul Asylum. There! That was easy. Turnoffs: Uh, fake people?

The first piece of lingerie was something Pasha was excited to put me in. "It's called a 'shelf,' " she said. "It's the sexiest thing ever. Really, supersexy." The shelf was a stiff sateen thing with a delicate wild-strawberry pattern, like a high corset, or a bustier without the *ier.* The breasts are pushed up by an unseen device and are meant to look displayed on a shelf, like two fresh sourdough loaves at the bakery, hoping to stow away in your picnic basket for the day. But when I tried it on, Pasha frowned. If you're too small for the shelf, the shelf backfires. In the mirror I was met with a new set of eyes staring back at me from my torso. Accusing, all-seeing eyes.

Pasha threw together a slapdash mix of frilly odds and ends: thigh-high stockings, various ivory-toned doilies, peach-colored ribbons and bows, and I was brought out to the set to be touched up in the light. Having makeup applied to your inner thighs in a roomful of people was just something I had to put out of my mind. I had to close my eyes and think of Sherman Oaks, let my soul hover above my body, pretend this was happening to someone else. I knew it wasn't how Pasha imagined her life, either. "Someday," she probably thought, "he'll ride up on a white horse and put a ring on my finger and take me away from all this, and we'll be Mr. and Mrs. Donald Mordechai Henley forever after." Good fucking luck, sister. Everyone knows you can't put Henley in a cage. Eagles gotta soar.

The set was a big, old-fashioned four-poster bed, angled, with caramel-colored satin sheets rippling over the edges and some incidental old-time props. (Angled beds must make readers want to fuck more. If your bed is in an unorthodox position, they assume, it must mean you are a free thinker who likes to give head.) I think it was meant to look inviting—a warm and sexy asylum against the autumnal chill, but to me, the set looked like a holding area concocted by the aliens who had taken me back to their planet to be studied. Trying to mimic my Earth surroundings as closely as possible, but working off just what they knew from old westerns, they adorned it with things they thought might amuse and comfort me: an old-fashioned hairbrush, and a hand mirror, in case the Earth girl wants to look at herself. Pasha adjusted my barely there, frontierswoman camisole so that it fell off one shoulder, and made my brown waves cascade down my back, as if the camera had caught me just after I'd undone my plaits. Overall, the motif conjured images of *Dr. Quinn, Medicine Woman,* after hours.

I took my place in front of the bed, and the assistant who had been sitting in for me stepped aside. There was no big reveal, no Coco in *Fame* tears; it wasn't like that. It was business. You are already nude and no one cares. You simply do what the photographer tells you to do, and you lose yourself in the adult contemporary soft rock.

Out on the road today I saw a Deadhead sticker
On a Cadillac . . .

Hang on, could that possibly be playing again? The music must've been on a loop. I looked for Pasha to see her reaction, but she and the assistant were sharing a laugh and imitating the last test girl, who had, unprompted, jutted her legs apart while lying on her back. They laughed about her, and I laughed to myself. Yeah, that girl was a piece of shit.

Richard Fegley shot roll after roll, saying very little except that I looked like a young Loretta Young. Who was that? The only Loretta I knew of was Loretta Lynn, and most of what I knew of her was what I had seen in Crisco commercials, where her family gathers around her big batch of fried chicken, and she says something like, "Dewey! Get in here and have some of this mess of chicken I jess fried up in this here Crisco shortening, and whatnot!" Or was it, "Dang you, Dewey, get your mitts off this here chicken, it's for Sundee dinner"? Why was she mad at him? I couldn't remember. Didn't Dewey used to beat her? She was the coal miner's daughter. I remember reading about her in my mom's *Family Circle* magazine. The one with the upside-down ice cream cones decorated like clowns for a child's party on the cover. That magazine always had upside-down ice cream cones on the cover, but for the October issue they were decorated like witches, and the cone was the hat.

Clowns, witches. Hmmm, I started to wonder, what other hats could you make out of ice cream cones?

Then someone yelled, "Lunch!"

An assistant had come around to take orders earlier, but I hadn't been provided with a menu, or even the name or type of restaurant. Was this because I should select something universal, or was it because I could have anything my heart could dream up? What shall I have, then? What do people have? What did Bebe Buell have? Peach yogurt, served in a diaphragm with a side of dry melba toast? But I panicked and ordered what everyone else had ordered: salad. Now in a robe, I collected the white cardboard container with my name on it, and I looked around for someone I could give money to, but everyone said it was cool, I could just hold on to my ten dollars. No one besides my mom had ever paid for my lunch before, and I didn't know quite how to take it.

After lunch, I was sent for a touch-up. Stepping into the makeup room, I caught Pasha on the phone, leaving Don a message. He must've been on the other line, ordering whores.

Back on set, I reclined against the gleaming bed. I was still bottomless and shoeless, but now the tattered rag I wore on top was stretched tight and tied in front, as if I were a hausfrau in a Benny Hill sketch. It was during this phase that I came closer to anything like a seductive pose: my gray-stockinged legs parted ever so slightly, my head cocked, and my expression devious, as if to say, "*Guten Abend,* gentlemen, come inside. I am the ex–peasant girl here to entertain you high-ranking officers of the SS."

And then it was over. I swabbed myself with baby wipes, got dressed, thanked everyone, and said good-bye. I couldn't wait to get in the shower—I still had some slashes of tawny orange in some places—and I was tired. Nudity is tiring, I had learned. So many feelings arise, but your mind has nowhere to put its hands. But I had done my best. I had stood there that day, nude, agitated, and very polite. I was barely legal, sweet, tumultuous, tempestuous, and conscientious. I hoped I had come off like the horny man's Loretta Young. All there was left to do now was go home and wait for a fan letter from J. D. Salinger.

None of my coworkers wanted to talk about my *Playboy* photo session. Kelly, Sarah, and I usually put our lipstick on together in the bathroom, on our way out for some after-work drinks, but lately they seemed to already have their lipstick on when it was time to go. One slow Saturday night, John, a dark but jovial twenty-three-year-old who also played drums in a local band, sat next to me behind the counter. "Now, why did you do this?" he asked. "Well," I said without hesitation, "I've always worried that I wasn't pretty enough, and even though people have said I am, I'm never sure. But if I got picked, it would mean, yes, I am good enough and pretty enough, even to someone who doesn't know me. See," I continued, averting my eyes from the dirty duct tape that held together the side seams of his suit, "I have bad, low self-esteem, and this helps me feel better about myself."

"Huh, that's inneresting," he said, rubbing his hands and wincing. He had sore fingers a lot. "Most people would have just said money."

Yes, there was that. The centerfold paid $15,000. That could buy a lot of Crabtree & Evelyn rosewater lotion, that was for sure. And a lot of Matte Mocha lipstick from the Soap Plant down the street. I could buy Heidi her freesia stuff she liked so much. I could shellac my Karmann Ghia in Man Ray postcards if I felt like it.

Weeks went by, and there was no word from *Playboy.* I carried on much like before, ringing up records, and reading *To the Lighthouse,* wearing silly little dresses, but I felt different somehow. Thirstier. It had been awhile since Heidi and I had made one of our midnight trips to the supermarket around the corner to buy beverages. We liked to push the cart home, and then proudly update our refrigerator list, but lately I'd been staying out late to drink with my Melrose friends. We'd drive around in Kelly's convertible, and John would wear a funny cap and shout, "Look at me! I look like fucking Dion!" and our shrieks of delight bounced all through the canyon.

One night, I stood in the doorway looking into Heidi's room. She'd always lamented her bright decor and favored the subtlety of my cool hues and framed, autographed posters of the Church, which was *her* favorite band to begin with. Her loud posters and colorful jungle sheets only served to enhance the garishness. Sometimes, when she'd cry, I'd think, "Oh, how sad to have to feel that way in there." It was bad enough for her—having to leave college—but next to the mocking, jester mask faces of the Red Hot Chili Peppers, things seemed so much worse. Why didn't she take those things down? Their stupid, idiotic faces. But what did I know anymore? My room, with its white IKEA end tables, used to give me such a quiet sense of superiority. Now, I wasn't so sure. Maybe I needed a new comforter altogether.

I was home alone one afternoon when a letter arrived from Playboy Enterprises, International. I opened it. *Playboy* regretted to inform me. They regretted to inform me that I wouldn't have to hang out at the mansion, or get $15,000, and I'd have to figure out for myself if I was pretty or not. It wasn't their problem anymore.

However, they would keep me in mind for future special issues, and I was invited to purchase copies of my photos for two dollars each.

Back at *Playboy,* Richard Fegley and I looked at my proofs. My pictures were lovely, he said, and he helped me pick out some to buy. He told me he was constantly battling the magazine's two women editors. "You know how it is," he sighed, "they just want the big boobs." I couldn't believe two women would think like that, but I didn't yet understand business. "Look at this girl's face," he said, pulling out a proof sheet of a girl splayed against a beach rock in bathing suit bottoms. "This girl's face makes me sick." She had bleached hair and a savage tan, and looked something like Pia Zadora, or Markie Post from *Night Court,* or someone like that, anyone like that. This was a girl the magazine wanted him to test shoot. I don't know if either one of us ever really thought they would pick me. I was just an element of one photographer's rage against the machine, and I died for everyone's sins.

I selected fifteen photos, trying to pick a few good, straight-on face shots that I could crop in case I wanted to use them for a headshot, if I wanted to do some acting someday or something. They looked nice, I supposed, but I wasn't a Playmate. I was the wrong kind of girl. My test had been hand-me-down rags and uninspired scenarios. I had not owned my space, or done anything alluring. Nothing looked sexy in a *Playboy* way. Not even in a Dana Plato in *Playboy* way. My ass, for example, didn't read sexy to me. It looked, I don't know, functional.

Richard Fegley still shopped at the store now and then, and when he'd come in with his lovely Japanese wife, it was never weird. It was business. I got my pictures in the mail in a brown wrapper, and my mom thought I looked very pretty.

One night, when I came home from work, there was a message on my machine from Stephanie Barnett at *Playboy*. Did they want me back? A special issue, perhaps? Girls of Melrose? The Girls of California State Universities English Departments?

No, my $30 check had bounced. She needed payment in cash or money order immediately. I stood in the hallway, looking into Heidi's room. I had to cover my ears. The cackling from those grotesques was getting louder and louder in the soft Sherman Oaks night.

Richard Fegley died in 2001. Although he had moved to Chicago, when I see him in my mind, he is always in a convertible custard yellow Porsche 911, driving up Pacific Coast Highway. It is always 1978, and sometimes, there's a riderless horse on the beach.

The record store is gone, too, and in its place is a store

that sells nothing but vintage T-shirts that bear the names of camps for people who never went to those camps—camps whose rowboats and marshmallows have been trampled in the relentless march of time. For some reason, the idea of strangers' long-gone camps makes people laugh and laugh. Oh, they just fall all over themselves.

Todd moved in with his sick mother, Sarah is a writer on *That's So Raven,* and the Boys of Summer left a long time ago, but I can't help but hope that somewhere, maybe in a corner of the back room, behind a rack, on a still-purple-painted patch of floor, there might be a finger-smudged Sonic Youth jewel case, or sticky gelato spoon, to prove we had been there. The street used to be a beacon in the cultural ocean, and now, with its multitude of halter-top and low-rise-jean shops, I guess it still is. "I made you," I think, looking at the hordes of kids walking down Melrose as I drive to drop off some banana bread I baked for my lawyer, "I made you and I can break you."

A few years ago I showed my husband, Kenny, the *Playboy* pictures. Even though they looked largely as I remembered—although in some I had the woeful expression of a man who had lost his pants and was adjusting the empty wooden barrel he now wore in their place—I did notice something for the first time. In all of the standing shots, I had one clenched fist. Always one clenched fist. "Let's get rid of these," Kenny said. He didn't like to see me all done up like some nonexistent man's fantasy in caramel and peach. But we should save them, I protested. In fifty years—"Nah," he said, and we tore the prints up into a million pieces. And now, since the great *Playboy* warehouse fire of

'98, they really are gone forever. It was ironic—pieces of my body were all over, as my life was coming together. It really touched on a lot of themes, like women's roles, and inner happiness, and society. It was a metaphor for lots of things, at least that's how I planned to describe it to an editor at *O, The Oprah Magazine.*

But there would be plenty of time for pitching another day. For now, it was Valentine's Day, and we had rented *The Last Waltz* again. We threw the picture scraps away, and put some heated Brie and French bread on the silver tray my mom had given us. We put the tray in the middle of bed, and played the peacock feather game with little Navin, who was three months old and whose cottony baby fur was just starting to relax into its silky tabby stripes. Soon, he got tired and fell asleep on our feet. We sang along to "The Weight."

Of course, that was back in the early 2000s, when we still ate cheese.

THE DENG LETTERS

Deng. Light of my life, fire of my loins. My sin, my soul, Deng.

The single syllable trips off the tongue and falls flat on the concrete floor. De-ng-ng. In the morning he was Deng, plain Deng at the check-cashing place. He was Deng, just Deng in the kitchen. He was Deng in pleats. At 5 P.M., hanging around the metal vats of raw chicken, he was still Deng. In the evenings, out on deliveries in the company Stanza, he was the Delivery Guy who tears your slip and gets a small tip. At the end of the night, lingering at the metal vats of raw pork, constantly harangued by the chef—Deng again. But with me, he was always Deng.

Maybe it was bold of him, an eighteen-year-old Thai immigrant who delivered food from a Thai restaurant and knew English only as it read in the window of his electronic pocket translator, to try to woo me, a twenty-four-year-old Caucasianness of some standing from the hills of eastern

Sherman Oaks. After all, I had once dined with Aidan Quinn *and* his agent. I used skin and hair products made by Kiehl's, and I slept so often past the noon hour. But he was possessed of a heart, a Dengish heart, and I broke it. Splintered it like the edges of the to-go chopsticks. Melted it like the handle of the plastic paddle that was left on the side of the rice cooker. Shattered it like some thin, hand-blown colored glass that has no place in the busy restaurant of reality.

It began in Santa Monica, California, where parking costs more, but the curbs are worth less. Santa Monica is the city around Santa Monica Beach, a very direct and level beach with no sex appeal.

In 1965, my family got in its car in Michigan and got out when they hit the Pacific Ocean. They were in Santa Monica. They ate at a family restaurant called Penguins, which had a big California penguin on the roof. Now it's a credit dentist's office, though the big penguin is still there. I wonder how many new settlers come out west and are delighted when they see it. "You see?" they turn and say to their clan. "In California, even the penguins can finance dental care!" And everyone nods their heads and agrees it was worth all the sacrifices it took to get there.

Having no plan and no work, my dad set the family up in a cheap motel in Santa Monica. I doubt in their wildest dreams they ever thought that one day, they'd have another daughter who'd grow up and work for six months in a Thai restaurant about thirteen blocks away. But then, who could have imagined such things? Such things were beyond imagination.

Then came the nineties, and with them, the era of the

nonthreatening Asian chef. Everywhere, stark, square plates of minimal Asian dishes were happening. Oh, what a time to be an Asian chef! People thought he was adorably exotic, and were very pleased when he wore the little chef pants in the crazy Jackson Pollock paint drip design and the Kangol cap. He just had such a fun take on things, and his minimalist approach applied not only to food, but also to life. The Asian chef delighted all with the wizardry of his fusion. He could fuse Asian flavors with just about anything. Even ideas.

Around this time, a white man who was a great fan of rock music met a Thai chef at Buddhism class and the two of them opened a restaurant in Hollywood called Pran: Rockin' Thai. It aimed to attract hungry rock stars, friends of rock stars, rock enthusiasts, the rock curious, general rockin' people, people who liked decadence, were badass, into Buddhism. Cool people, who liked sugar-free organic tarts, newcomers, oldgoers, and, of course, rockers. The owners decorated the place with leopard-print tablecloths, and *black* carpet, and covered every inch of wall space with Jimi Hendrix posters and other kickass things. They staffed it with hot waitresses who could almost be models, kept it open until 4 A.M., and invited everyone to come and sit on the floor and eat pad Thai all night under the twinkling guitars.

Everything was going so great that one day, the owners of Pran: Rockin' Thai looked around their purple, black, and leopard jewel and realized they had a problem. Buddha had blessed them with abundance, all right—an abundance of INXS posters, for one thing! The walls were so crowded with paraphernalia that there wasn't room for even an inch more rock.

The two wise men thought and thought. I think they thought, "Hey, Rockin' Thai seems to be going well, people are responding to the melding of rock and roll and Asian flavors here in Hollywood. Maybe we should open another place on the west side, say, Santa Monica?" They decided they thought it was a great idea. Plus, it was closer to Buddhism class.

But then it hit them: Santa Monica was a place of chambray shorts and decent bedtimes. The shopping carts were shiny and new. The windows had flower boxes. *Kempt* flower boxes. Rock and rollers don't have flower boxes! Santa Monica was too priggish for Rockin' Thai, too set in its ways. The two men of two different cultures but one common goal thought and thought. They split a barley-sweetened organic tart, and stopped thinking for the day.

But the next day, when they got together to think, they hit on the best idea in the whole world: *jazz Thai.*

Jazz was to Santa Monica what rock was to Hollywood. A location was chosen.

Concurrently, mysterious cargo ships were traveling from the Far East. When certain ships reached the California shore, after eighteen days or so, and the bribed officials opened the crates and the survivors breathed the soft, salty Southern California air, they said to their clans, "You see? I told you! In California, we can finance our debt to the coyotes by preparing and delivering Asian food!" And they all agreed it was worth all the sacrifices it took to get there.

A lady chef, Tuk, manned the new place, but she was

large and brusque and delighted no one. The sexy waitress spillover from the original restaurant was installed. My grouchy, spiritual roommate, Tara, was one.

I had abandoned college by this point, dropped out to reinvestigate becoming an actress, but a comic actress this time. Most of my week was spent in comedic acting classes, coming up with characters and writing sketches, but I still found so many outlets for my weekly fifty-dollar check from Mom and Dad. I really needed a job. Tara pointed me westward, to Pran.

I met the white guy, Rex, who was gray-haired and black-jeaned. Success had left him blasé, powdery. He asked if I had any experience. I told him I had worked (lie) in my mom's restaurant (lie) and he said it was cool with him if I worked there.

To be a waitress at Pran carried with it a dash of mystique. It meant you were less than a model, but more than a waitress. I had never waitressed or had any kind of job in the food service industry. My repulsion at the idea of other people's food—their disgusting, sauce-smeared plates, sullied forks, and lip-moistened remains—had kept me thus far firmly stationed in counterculture retail. I had never cleared another's plate, grazed another's chilly leftovers with my thumb. I still dislike the idea of people eating, the whole concept of service. One person serving another person. It just makes me shudder.

While dining on location in Asheville, North Carolina, two fellow comedy writers and I got on the topic of gratuities. It was one of those loose, luxurious nineties conversations, except that it took place in 2005. Jermaine and I, although both big tippers, were of the mind that tipping is an exploitative, outdated convention. He and I grew up instinctively rejecting these tenets of the Establishment: servitude, positive attitudes, authority, the conditions on Maggie's farm, being judged by strangers, going through proper channels, Florida orange juice, God, teachers, the Capitol Steps, jellied hams, Nurse Ratched, uniforms, Dell computers, back-to-school value days, calcium, fertility drugs, height requirements, and standardized tests. My six-month stint at Pran notwithstanding, Jermaine and I were classic nonwaiters. My summer job had always been Affected Independent Record Store Clerk. I don't know about Jermaine's early jobs, but I'm sure he did some kind of angry strawberry picking or disenchanted collating or other.

Abel, on the other hand, thought "the tip should reflect the quality of service and served as an incentive to do a good job." Wow.

His summer job? Waiter.

"But how can you . . . what business is it . . . whore yourself . . . shouldn't have to . . . there should be a system in place . . . so don't you feel . . . it's not up to . . . didn't you . . . degrading to assume . . ."

Oh, it was useless. Abel was a pleasant guy who always gave two quick knocks on your car hood as you drove away.

That said, I liked waitressing. I gave in to the nice feeling I got from bringing a person something he or she liked to eat and then getting a little treat right afterward that I could put straight into my pocket. Every weekday, a small crowd of ill-tempered loners came in for the $4.50 lunch specials.

They'd all leave a five-dollar bill on the table and rarely say thank you, but not even that fazed me. I even became impervious to the sight of abandoned plates with their revolting little egg rolls all in ruins. I fluttered around with a pen in my hair and made light jokes.

Besides the cubicle crowd, no one ate at Pran: Jazz Thai. The menu was the same standard-issue Thai with a few fusions ("Thai Spaghetti" was one) and some somber rice/squash bowls—but this location had none of the built-in sexy of the Hollywood place. That place was old, had architectural flourishes. This place was a new small square with a drop ceiling. Its vibe was at one with the surrounding doughnut shops and P.O. box places. The walls were white, there was a counter. The chairs were black with gray fabric. There were tablecloths. Everything looked like it had just come from an Armenian Association Steering Committee brunch. Rex and the Chef had to figure out a way to literally jazz the place up.

Every day or so, some new jazz element arrived at Pran. A pair of papier-mâché musical notes up front were there to set the *tone.* Everything was moving in a bright, multicultural, jazzular direction. "Hey, look at that awesome photo of Satchmo!" the west-side diner was supposed to say. "Man, that cat was smooth, just like this coconut-based soup," to which the west-side companion might come back with, "Lemongrass is so fragrant. Hey, don't you think Miles Davis was the essence of cool?" That was the hope, anyway.

The place was looking like a Cosby sweater; the local, community-supported jazz station *zoobeedoobieedoo*'ed from

the speakers, but still no vibe, no fusion, no melding of flavors. When Rex came by to bring new art, or check on past
art, he was inevitably met with an empty or emptying
room. He speculated that maybe the waitresses weren't
doing enough to bring in business and once, very dryly and
ponytailedly, suggested that we girls needed to start "dancing on the tables." Why, Rex? Why suggest that? It wasn't
going to make you twenty-five again. Nothing would. Not
even your band.

(Purple Crosses was their name, and he'd inserted their
"record covers" and shameful, hand-lettered flyers into
the rock-mantled walls of the other restaurant, as if someone might accidentally think, "Yeah, I love all those bands,
Led Zeppelin, the Who, Purple Crosses." I'd heard that
the West Hollywood employees were even made to go to
Purple Crosses shows. How sad a scene it must've been:
the obligatory lineup after the show to tell the boss how
much he "rocked.")

More knickknacks were called for, and more knickknacks were brought in. Local artists were commissioned
to create work that would connote a vibe, any vibe. Any
vibe at all. Anyone with ties to either the jazz or Pacific
Rim community was encouraged to petition to the owners
for art space.

A fellow waitress, Diane, and I thought the whole thing
very funny.

"Okay, how 'bout a photo of a saxophone, like, in some
negative space, all shiny and everything, with a bunch of
pad Thai coming out of it?"

"Black-and-white?"

"Absolutely," I said, "a black-and-white art photograph, and down at the bottom it would say 'The Flavor of Jazz,' but wait, it'd be spelled out in noodles!"

"Or," she laughed, "it could be curry, like a spicy red curry, like, coming out of a trumpet or something, and it could say 'Spicy Hot Jazz!' "

Now I was dying. "No, wait! It'd say 'Red Hot 'n' Jazz' and it would be written in curry sauce!"

"And, and! The z's would be red chilies!"

With Thai iced coffee dribbling from the corners of her mouth, Diane ducked her head into the sink and let it all fall. These art jokes were almost as funny as her suggestion to improve business by offering notary public services with every lunch special. This was the only joy we got at Pran: the hour when the lunch waitress and the dinner waitress shifts overlapped, and Diane and I were grateful for the bright spot between two gigantic gulfs of solitude. I was glad she was covering the shifts of Amelia, the suspicious blond waitress from the Bay Area who was studying to get her masseuse license, and was recently found to be living in the kitchen storage closet at night and licking great handfuls of hallucinogens. She always seemed odd to me, and lately, it had been noted by some of the staff that she smelled a bit off, like a mix of dirty rags and cardamom. I remember the morning they found her, wrapped only in a tie-dyed T-shirt, going on and on about some kind of lymph-draining elephant gods.

Working with the girls who weren't Diane was less fun. I received my original training from serious, faraway Caroline, the first and most adept of the team. She knew the menu intuitively, as if coconut milk ran in her veins. With her buzzed hair like a cap of chestnut velvet and her delicate South African accent, she glided through the tables like a splendid mare. She was famous for working an entire Hollywood Friday night alone and making $80 in tips. How on earth did she do it? Eighty dollars! She waitressed on another level.

I was not so capable. Never during my tenure was I able to differentiate between the dishes at Pran. Some lady would ask, "What's in the Pad Poh Tak?" and I'd subtly crane my head down toward the menu in her hands and read the description back to her aloud. No one ever noticed. They didn't really care about the answer anyway. They wanted to learn some ethereal truth that's not on a menu. They wanted assurance of some kind, not about the food, just assurance of some sort. They needed to know, if they ordered the Pad Poh Tak, would things change? Would the energy in Pad Poh Tak propel their consciousness beyond this moment in this drop-ceilinged restaurant? Would they have chosen the right path? Or did the yellow curry have better powers?

There were a few loyalists: people who'd come in alone wearing layers of hand-dyed scarves who knew what they wanted. Those orders were easy. I'd write down "EPT": Eggplant. Pumpkin. Tofu. And an "LBR," large brown rice. They also wanted a glass of tepid water, or even an empty glass to pour their own water into, or just a cup with some hot water into which they'd place their own tea bag from home. They sat and read (Carlos Castaneda, always) and existed in that moment, on that plane, devoid of earthly wants, aware that they were one with the Universal Mind. They took home their leftovers, no bag, thank you, for they had brought their own bamboo storage containers for this purpose.

I had a fantastically hard time differentiating between the more elaborate dishes on the Pran menu, especially the ones I didn't give a crap about. Boredom led me to try most everything they served, and as hot as the kitchen would make it. I liked for my discounted evening meal to order the noodles, or certain curries, but never, ever with the special brown rice. It was the pride of Pran, called "black rice," which was more of a bruise purple and so jammed with nutritional gravel that no amount of peanut sauce could smooth it down. I also stayed far away from the thing they called "Thai BBQ Chicken" and I had only ever seen a "Seafood Bird's Nest" once. (It was on my first night while I was trailing Caroline. I remember how gently she brought it out from the kitchen so as not to disturb the thorny masterpiece of a deep-fried noodle nest doused in soupy clams and things. "I'll never get the hang of this," I thought, on a cigarette break in the alley.)

There was no rigid dress code at Pran. You could wear whatever pants you pleased as long as the fabric cradled the landscape of your ass in such a way that it appeared around the undercurve like a ripe, tantalizing peach. No jeans. And no tennis shoes of any kind.

Every night I came home to the big, prewar apartment on Sixth Street that I shared with too many other girls. I'd have miserable, aching feet, the kind you hear about in folklore. Had I been like Linda Lavin's character on the TV show *Alice,* my precocious son, Tommy, would've poured hot water into a basin for me to soak away the day's toll. But I wasn't Linda Lavin's character on the TV show *Alice* and I had no one to do that for me.

At home I had Renata, the actress, who always made sure there was enough whole-bean, intense, shade-grown coffee in the pantry to strip the enamel off all our young teeth, and Andie, who got the private bathroom because she found the place. She was a great découpager of end tables. She was possessed of a trust fund and loved spirituality nearly as much as Tara, who lived for a time in the hollow of the office nook. She was very sensitive to the magic inherent in the world's children.

Even I fell into the spirit life for a time. I went to a chain nature store, the kind that sells rain sticks in malls, and I had my young niece select some colored stones for me to keep on my nightstand to rub and fondle and cry on before falling asleep and dreaming. I thought they would be more powerful because they were chosen by a child, whose spirit hath more purity than mine. I've always been too willing to absorb into other people's minds, styles, vibes.

The two of them, Andie and Tara, were forever aching to have congress with ghosts. It was practically all they ever talked about. Renata and I sat and made mental lists of the minor celebrities we wanted to try to screw while the other two hovered around the walls and felt for spooky vibrations. One would come home from a job (Rockin' Thai, in Tara's case) and the other would be all atwitter about the day's cold spots or shadow patterns. The dining room, I recall, was a real hotbed of activity, possibly some kind of portal. Then, one evening in January 1994, Tara brought home a Psychic Circle. A Psychic Circle was a Ouija board, but circular, and updated for the nineties Wicca-curious, not made by Parker Brothers, and with richer colors. She must've gotten it at the Bubble Bubble Toil and Trouble Witch Supply & Feed Company just outside of town.

We four roommates convened in Andie's room and arranged ourselves around the circle. Tara was mystically eager. Andie was metaphysically yearning. Renata and I had some questions we wanted to ask about guys and fucking. We each placed a hand on the pointer and looked at each other.

After about an hour, the pointer seemed like it was possibly heading toward the letter *R,* but it was still too soon to tell. Renata ran to answer the phone in her room, visibly annoying Tara. She came back and announced that Stephen Dorff was having some people over to his bungalow at the Chateau Marmont. How stupid, we thought, and went about readying ourselves, leaving the two witchy women hunched over the circle. As we left the apartment, we heard them summoning the newly dead River Phoenix from eternal rest.

"Say hi to River for us," we called out, but they didn't answer.

That night was the Northridge Quake. At 4:30 A.M., we were all thrown up against walls and out of beds. Andie initially thought the Circle caused it, and that it only happened in her room.

These were not the people to ease my aches, feet or otherwise.

I didn't have the right shoes, as usual. Never one for a broad toe box, I always chose delicate shoes with softly tapering fronts and usually a little stable height in the back. And while my shoes weren't Lucite icicle stripper heels, they weren't waitress-worthy. Waitress Danielle told me what all waitresses knew—that I should get myself a pair of regular Doc Martens.

Doc Martens? No way. Maybe in '83, but not now. And not even in '83. Back then, I only wore punk shoes that had pointy toes and buckles. Shoes that said "Yes, I hate the Establishment, but I'm still a lady." I didn't wear punk boy shoes then, and I certainly wasn't about to wear post-grunge-just-knocking-around-the nineties-waiting-for-the-next-Cameron-Crowe-movie-to-come-out shoes now.

But my feet really hurt, so I submitted. I bought the shoes (in black), I laced them up and tried to enjoy myself. And do you know what? The pain subsided.

And perhaps it was those things: the mending of an ache, my submission to clunky shoes, the willingness to serve, to throw my head back and laugh a little while doing so; that tiny new light just turned on, which attracted the ever-patrolling moth of Deng's fancy.

There is no other way to say this: Deng looked like a piece of propagandist art from World War II: skinny, slack, with a massive Adam's apple, jutting front teeth, and a ragged bowl haircut. I say this as a person whose kind have often been illustrated as miserly rodents, for whatever that's worth. Besides, I doubt many Thai people will read this. My stuff doesn't really *skew* Thai.

Deng'd show up every day around five, stand around

the kitchen, get yelled at by the Chef, hold out his arms to be loaded with brown paper bags, drive off in the Nissan Stanza, come back, get other paper bags, drive off, come back, get yelled at for forgetting a bag or taking too long.

We didn't get along at first, Deng and I. Following the lead of kitchen staff, who were cold to new waitresses at first, and most of the time after that, Deng found cause to reprimand me whenever he could. "Not what ordered!" he'd shout, pointing a long, slim finger at a disgraced delivery slip. Old Pass-the-Buck Deng. Good old Misplaced Aggression Deng. What did he want from me? That's what the people had said on the phone. He also had it in his head that the waitress, not the kitchen staff, and certainly not he, was supposed to pack up the to-go orders, and even though he was right, he was unable to communicate to me why this was to happen, and thus it never did.

He was unable to communicate to me his frustration, and I was unable to communicate to him that I didn't care, and somehow, we must've reached an understanding of this because he eventually stopped shaking his head at me.

When I was getting ready to leave one night, under the empty jug of Thai tea starter concentrate, which he knew I'd be refilling, the dickens, I found a lovingly folded piece of college ruled notebook paper. Inside was written:

★The Report Heart★

Dear Stacy★

I, will speak thinking fo you. but impossible I. Have say sorry toyou. I can't speak and answer has understanding English not tomuch And I. don't know you can have friend

147

thailand And Awerse me. I, have sincerity for you today and liflong. Don't have word lie from me.

I, come from country the small one. and rube I. have word upright for you one only And I. hope next year have you gotomy country And I. will crook you engage with ring diamond and I, hope marry for next time I., want tell you everytime I. am like you So much And I, don't thing you will forget me and hate me I. don't have learning and impose from you i. love you with my hant and have Somany can not tell you.

When I. can speak good English. I, will do everything for you. This is a word from the one man. I. am swear have you Forever.

thank you,
phongsak

I didn't want to believe it, but it was all right there in the Report Heart. Clear as day. He am swear have me forever.

I don't think I ever spoke to Deng more than was necessary to relieve boredom and privileged-girl guilt. I always said hello and good-bye and made small talk, and I recall him teaching me the one Thai phrase I wanted to know: *nakH saL daaen dtaL lohkL*—"comic actress." I was friendly to him, but no friendlier than I was to Tuk, the Chef, or the dishwasher, and neither of them wanted to crook engage me. Crook, maybe, but not engage.

I didn't provoke him, if that's what you're thinking!

If that's what you're thinking, you can just get that thought out of your head right now!

After showing the letter to most of my friends, and

reading it aloud over the phone to the rest, I sat down and had a long hard talk with myself about how best to handle this delicate situation.

I remembered some old advice I'd heard a lady on TV say. She said, "Look here, missy, when something's bothering you, just pretend it didn't happen and go about your business." "Well," I thought, "if it could work with that flasher behind McDonald's, it could certainly work here."

I pretended like nothing had happened, and that worked beautifully for me. But Deng kept staring, and staring. There I'd be, serrated knife in hand, sawing into a barley-sweetened tart, seeing how many espressos I could make and drink in an hour, folding the cloth napkins into vulgar shapes, minding my own business, and there he'd be, slumped pitifully in the pink glow of the neon clarinet, his clumsy love practically bursting through the worn nylon of his fanny pack.

I'd pray for lots of deliveries to places at the edge of the delivery zone map.

Inevitably, the starchy-smelling daughters of the kitchen staff started encircling my front counter. Until now, they always stayed out of the way, stationed on plastic crates, sweetly doing their homework with fancy hologram pencils all night, but news of Deng's crush emboldened them. Two or three at a time would tiptoe out, giggling, tap me on the hip, run away, run back, giggle, and scamper off. Then another would appear and uncup her mouth long enough to say, "He thinks [*tee-hee-hee*] you are lovely!" before breaking into full-faced laughter and running off. We couldn't stand them, Deng or I.

He had his own way of telling me things. I'd find little notes everywhere that said things like: "Stacy=lovely" and "Hello!"

One bleak Santa Monica late afternoon, after I had dried every utensil in the gray plastic bin and lit all the little votives on the tables, which I'd reset all in the Pran dinner style with the little napkins in the middle of the groovy plate with the red chopsticks placed horizontally along the top, I sat down behind the counter with a plate of white rice and peanut sauce. Deng was, again, stationed at the table with the clearest view of me, where he'd be all night.

A minute later, the owners came in with a big group. Rex strutted Zenly, as only a restaurateur in a T-shirt and blazer could. The Chef jauntily sat everyone. His swift movements made his Keith Haring pants bloom like tea bags.

I knew who these people were.

The Westside Buddhists were the roughest, toughest congregation in town and this was their clubhouse. They swarmed the place, pivoting chairs around to sit in them backward, slapping people on the backs of their heads. Besides the two owners, there was Abe, a balding, serene self-publisher of poems about the pleasures of sobriety. He molested everyone he ever met. There was Mackenzie Phillips, who had played Julie on *One Day at a Time*. A noted badass, you didn't want to mess with her. And then you had Gomez, from *The Addams Family*, various Buddhist goons, and some brightly shrouded holy men who were probably pretty high up the chain.

The best thing was to try to be invisible to the Buddhists. The less they had to know you existed, the better.

Just be fast and don't fuck anything up. Wear your Doc Martens. Don't talk to the Buddhists beyond what is necessary. Give them whatever they ask for. Never tell them no or try to engage them. If they throw something on the floor or at the wall, pretend you don't see it. Don't clean it up until after they're gone.

Shit! Was Caroline still here? I remember her mindfully finishing up some EPT and an LBR and saying something to the plate about how she'd miss all the beautiful colors in the world, and then I guess she left. Shit! I couldn't do this! I had made and drunk eleven espressos in the last two hours.

Rex and the Chef seemed agitated, and there was so much noise, so much hollering and whooping. Nor did it help that Deng, parked in his usual spot with the counter view, still wouldn't stop staring at me!

And then,

Hot water burn Julie!
Hot water burn Julie!

I had spilled hot eggplant-pumpkin water all over Julie from *One Day at a Time*. It crinkled and scorched her thin skirt fast to her thigh.

The Chef chuckled vehemently, and sprung up for kitchen towels. The Buddhists banged the table, whooped and cackled like furious cranes, but all I heard was the silence of the edge of Rex's gray pageboy skimming the collar of his collarless shirt as he turned his aged face to me.

Her thigh. The things that thigh had lived through!

Encased in brown corduroy, it had cantered in the Hollywood fast lane, picking up speed as teen Mackenzie fevered for more and more drugs. The thigh knew obscure Mamas and Papas facts. The thigh, all too often, came home ashamed with the rising sun. And now to those assaults I had added injury. The juice was kitchen-hot enough to sear her skirt pattern to her skin like the atomic bomb blasts had done with kimonos of the Japanese. This unforgettable fire would be just one more thing for the Phillips thigh to overcome.

Mackenzie took the bowl, and what remained in it, and set it before her on the table. Then she reached up and with both hands took my elbow and pulled me in closer. All around, people were dabbing her lap with cloth. She paid them little notice.

Her eyes boring into my eyes, she said, "It's okay. No, really, don't worry about it. It's nothing. No, honestly. No, it's fine. I'm totally fine."

Was she?

Was she really?

The days continued to break and end, break and end, and my little white Nissan continued on its long path to and from Santa Monica. Weeks went by. At least two.

One day, Rex grooved on through the front door, just like Joe Cool, and started doing his Rex things: fingering the depth of cash in the register drawer, inspecting things, making the presence of his blazer felt.

"What's wrong with him?" asked Rex about silent Deng, who didn't seem to care that he was slumping forward in such a way that the back of the chair was cutting into his Adam's apple. Every day that I did not respond to his marriage proposal must've plucked another vertebra from his spine.

I pretended not to know what was with him, but one of his countrymen sold Deng out.

I discreetly, yes, discreetly, showed Rex a copy of The Report Heart (not the original—that was on exhibit at my friend Ben's house for the month of October). He shook his gray pageboy. "Oh man," he said. We laughed about it a little, and by way of conversation I said if I ever got "rich and famous" I was going to frame the letter and put it in my bathroom. Who knows why? I suppose those were the kinds of things I said in 1995. It made no sense. Frames are not that much, I had nails, and I had a bathroom already. What prompted me to say such things?

Still, Rex said it was "not cool" for him to bother the waitresses. That he was the only one who was allowed to bother the waitresses, heh heh.

The next morning, not even concealed by the decency of an empty Thai tea jug, was this note:

Dear Stancy

I. beg you pardon for perturb and do the bother for you. I. hook Understanding and you my aim I. don't understand why American peppel Say word berate. I. know now you has mind narrow I. beg tell you Associate and Somecorrect I, don't have you for marry or for girl friend. you mistake because I, I will marry next year and thai girl. 2 I. associate don't hope aught I, do for you good friend and for Speak English. I, don't thinq you have habit Indecent I, lnow now you don't like friend From Asian because poor and Surface yellow—Same me. I, will tell you never mind, you don't like see me and next time you need Some help please tell me. I feel great Sorrow for you Speak.

> *DENG*

So now I was a racist.

How silly of me to think his offer to crook and engage me with ring diamond and marry for next time was an offer to crook and engage me with ring diamond and marry for next time. Obviously, *I* mistake. Me and my habits indecent, I had imagined the whole thing. What a fool I was, what a narrow-minded fool. He felt great sorrow for me speak. *He* felt great sorrow for *me* speak.

Yet he still had the capacity to offer me help should I need it.

But was I the fool? No! Deng was. Deng was the fool! He was a proposal denier. A feelings revisionist. Gone was the trust that allowed him to share with me his proper name. He was Deng, again and for all time. I don't know why American peppel use word berate either! If you want to know the truth, I don't know why American peppel do a lot of things. Deng, you didn't do the bother for me, honestly! It was no bother! Oh, Deng, Deng, Deng, Deng, Deng . . . (Repeat, until the page is full, printer.)

Diane showed up in the late afternoon for those sixty minutes of overlapping shifts so I took a smoke vacation out in the alley.

The ocean fog felt like it was coming in. A Santa Monica day was softly becoming a Santa Monica night. Soon the ladies and their matching men would finish their strolls and change out of their chambray shorts into something more appropriate for an evening at home watching Sela Ward on television. The windows of the houses were starting to close, and the window-box flowers were curling into themselves. It was the Jazzing Hour.

Maybe I should've said yes.

Yes to Deng, yes to Thailand, yes to Life.

Our wedding would be a grand spectacle. I'd wear a dress of lotus petals and rice paper, and Deng would wear the ceremonial silk wedding cloak of his ancestors (all kings), but he'd adorn a buttonhole with a tiny paper American flag in my honor. There'd be coconut cake.

I'd be the greatest comic actress Thailand had ever seen. They'd call me "Chaaem Phuu"—The Lovely One—and my sixteen handmaidens would bathe me in the milk of only the youngest coconuts to keep my skin as milky white as the youngest coconuts. And in the morning, golden-finger-tipped dancing maidens, sixteen of them, for some reason, would perform the Morning Dance in my honor. Later, the Afternoon Dance. Midday would come and also, in my honor, the Three O'Clock Dance, followed by the Dinner Dance and the Midnight Dance. Then they would do for me the Dawn Dance, but they'd do it before I went to bed, because they knew I didn't like to get up for the Dawn Dance. Oh, there'd be the New Moon Dance, and the Harvest, Equinox, and Back to School Dances. So many dances! So much coconut! Flowers, jewels! On painted elephants I'd ride.

I'd have all my special things delivered from the West,

and my private maid would tiptoe around them as she dusted and attended to my vanity of solid ivory. Once, I'd catch her caressing my special things. I'd stand and watch, grinning to myself, but she'd see me and gasp, and put her hands behind her back, and cast her eyes down in shame. "It's okay," I'd say. "You can touch." And I'd put the treasure back in her hand. "It's called 'Silk Groom,' and it's for your hair." Her eyes would fill with glee while she held my Kiehl's bottle. I'd put some in her hair. I'd guide her hand. "See, it tames flyaways and creates texture," and she'd giggle and run off down the hall to show the others.

And Deng would be a most attentive husband. We'd have six or seven cashew-colored children with sparkling green eyes and sardonic streaks. At last! The melding of our two cultures in living, breathing form! They'd all grow up to be extremely successful dance club promoters and day traders.

With all my free time, I'd be able to work on lots and lots of projects about my cross-cultural experience. Maybe I'd develop a monologue based on a series of articles about our relationship that I'd write for *Parade* magazine called "Apple Pie and Sticky Rice."

Which might then become the basis for a richly photographed and poignantly beautiful documentary about the struggle of a forgotten people that would be an official selection at Sundance called *So Many Cannot Tell You*. I'd get nominated for an Independent Spirit Award, and we'd fly out for the ceremony, and Deng would be there in the audience and people would point and say, "Oh, that's the real guy."

And through it all, he'd continue to write me one love letter a day, and his English would improve at the rate the sun dies.

Sometimes, I'd get frustrated and hide his electronic translator. He'd fire the maid for stealing, and I'd say nothing. More and more, I'd retire to my Internet chat rooms to unwind.

He'd wonder why I seemed so disinterested in my Thai lessons, and I'd attempt to appease him every now and then by asking how to say, "If there's a bustle in your hedgerow, don't be alarmed now," and that would put a temporary end to things. Eventually, I'd shout across the dining room table, "I'll never learn Thai. It is an inferior language. Proust didn't write in Thai!" knowing full well he didn't get the reference. I'd want to have intense debates about why you simply shouldn't have a jazz Thai or a rock Thai restaurant because English is the language of rock, and jazz is the only true American art form. I'd challenge him to name three great French rock bands, but he wouldn't be able to do it because it's impossible, and furthermore, he wouldn't know what I was talking about.

I'd grow weary of him.

And start to miss things from the old neighborhood. The LaBianca murder house. Things about America. Rock. Roll. Tumbleweeds.

He'd start to spend all his time nailing underaged prostitutes.

Then one day, while in town with my young girls, an American magazine with a picture of a huge American movie star on the cover would catch my eye and I'd stop to look at it. "Who is that?" my youngest would ask. "His eyes are so very blue, bluer than the Pa Sak River."

Yes, my love, they are.

"Who is it, *maan-daa*? Who is the American man?"

How would I explain these things to her? What could I tell my daughter about Aidan Quinn? I'd sigh an audible sigh and say, "It is no one, little one. No one." And I'd turn my face away.

At night, I'd tear out my eyelashes in sorrow, making wishes upon each one before sending it off into the sparkling Bangkok night.

By then, Diane had joined me in the doorway and lit her own cigarette. She noticed I was far away.

"Whatcha thinking about?"

I told her I was thinking about shoes.

And then, all at once, there was a flash of blazer. A torso burst out of the back door, and a voice shouted, so loudly: "WHAT THE FUCK ARE YOU DOING OUT HERE?"

Rex. Jesus.

One waitress smoking is okay, as long as the other is watching the front. But two waitresses smoking is not allowed.

Diane bowed her head and threw her cigarette down.

"WHAT THE FUCK IS WRONG WITH YOU?"

I felt a flutter along my side. It was the breeze created by Diane running back to her counter post, her "sorry's" trailing behind her. I stayed where I was. I was technically right.

"YOU BETTER GET YOUR ASSES BACK—"

And this is where I put a stop to things. I said, "Excuse

me?" (The Valley Girl's version of the cocking of a rifle.) "You do not talk to us that way. Ever. Not for any reason."

Rex told me he would talk any way he wanted. It was his restaurant and he owned it.

I said I didn't care, and that it was "not okay" to speak to us that way under any circumstances. And if he thought he was going to speak to *me* that way, he'd better think again.

And he said that I should just get the fuck out with that atti—

And I said, No fucking problem, I quit this place.

I grabbed my things, said good-bye to Diane, who said it was wrong of him, seriously wrong, stormed through the kitchen, glad I'd never again have to see the remnants of so many sweet and decent pigs that curdled in yellowy spices all day, and took to my Nissan.

I drove the long drive home in just my socks (the Doc Martens had gone in the first trash bin my little Nissan and I passed). I cursed, and ranted, and vowed, and said, "Excuse me?" aloud all the way home.

I said aloud, "Excuse me? Gomez? Is that all you've got? Gomez and Julie from *One Day at a Time*? You're going to have to do better than that if you want to *even try* to fuck with *me*, old man. Fuck your jazz hole. I hope it burns down in a grease fire."

I thought, "You nit. You cretin. You creep. The nerve of you. I'll get you, Rex Swanson. No matter what I have to do. If it takes me ten years, and I have to get a book deal from Scribner just to take you down, I will, Rex Swanson. I will. I never forget. I'll cut your guts out and cook them on high heat. I may not be a Buddhist, but this is my karma, or your karma. No one talks to me like that. I hold a grudge. Not some pussy jazz grudge, either, I hold a rock grudge. The kind of rock you'll never know. The kind Purple Crosses can't play. There are no collarless shirts in the rock of my grudge. I'll burn a big purple cross on the lawn of your mind, man, because I don't eschew revenge, I thrive on revenge. I relish the exposure of meanies and jerks! Revenge is not only sweet, it is an exotic, aromatic blend of sweet and savory, infused with tangy citrus."

If you were to go to Pran: Jazz Thai today, you'd find no trace of jazz. At some point, it switched to familiar territory: rock. Out went the member-supported local radio station, the neon sax; in came the Jim Morrison poster, the Ramones record clock. What changed? Has the world changed? At least in Santa Monica it has.

But one would do well to remember all the sacrifices it took to get it there. Sacrifices of all the Deng Panomyaongs out there, in beat-up Stanzas, bringing you the world in a paper bag with napkins and utensils.

And of those like me, whose quality of service will not necessarily be reflected in the size of the tip, but who must still endure the crown. I am condemned to walk this earth wearing a bird's nest of seafood upended on my head, its tangle of noodle thorns scraping my forehead as black mussels clamp onto wet strands of my hair and calamari tendrils curl into my eyes and crab, bits of crab, all over the fucking place, just to remind you all that you can't raise sea creatures in a bird's nest. They die.

ONE INDULGENT MELODY

On the eve of the week that was to birth the next millennium, the newest one, I was flying from Los Angeles to Chicago. All around me, people were talking, not just on the plane, but also in a grander sense, and from what I could gather, they were talking about Polarfleece. Polarfleece was one of the new extreme hybrid fabrics that had everyone enveloped in its warm spell. It was manufactured at the Earth's poles expressly for garments called "tech vests," which had special compartments for keeping all kinds of things. Millennial things, the latest exceedingly specialized tools that we'd carry with us into the 2000s, like a device that told you what restaurants were in the vicinity of the movie theater you were going to, and nothing more. (I couldn't wait to get one of those.) It was that transitory period in American history when there were still fewer people on TV than there were people not on TV. From the global subwoofers pulsed a constant hip flow of rap hop, sounding just as brisk and germane as it had in 1998. All along the coasts, Sephora beauty superstores were sprouting up, and many people either had their own fragrance lines, or were in talks to launch their own fragrance lines, and those who didn't at least had a barbecue sauce or assortment of Pacific Rim fusion marinades named for them, if I recall.

Kenny and I had been married a few months, and he had just shown me what a real Christmas experience was. For weeks before, thousands of dollars' worth of fleeting fashion were folded into boxes beneath our tiny tree, where they sat, cooing and fussing softly among themselves until the big day. These unfamiliar sounds took some time to get used to, like one's first nights in the country, but I would finally get to know what other people had been playing out every year—the reality of this thing, this "Christmas"—sinking deeply into debt and competing with your friends.

Soon I'd be landing at O'Hare, and then taking a rickety prop plane over Lake Michigan to eventually wind up in Grand Rapids. I was on assignment for the basic cable news parody show I worked on, a show that we all still called simply *The Daily Show,* but that official name had been changed to *The Daily Show with Jon Stewart* when the comedian Jon Stewart took over as host.

This was my second trip to "the Rapids," to use the term of Hollywood agents and other professionals. I was sent there on assignment a year earlier to meet a woman who had gained some local acclaim for making a Virgin Mary sculpture out of dryer lint. But it wasn't really what it had promised to be. The woman, whose name I have long since forgotten, had made as respectable a statue as one could out of dryer lint. She mixed it with liquid starch (which we didn't know beforehand) so it was basically a hardened papier-mâché construct that she then painted the appropriate Mary colors (blue, white). The show's producer, Chiara, and I stood dumbly in the Michigan living room of this wedge-haired housewife. We assumed, based on what we had been told, that a statue made out of dryer lint would look, well, like lint, but it just looked like any other thing that could be sold in the home section of Ross. This was more like a folksy human-interest story than a trek through the dusky creases of one woman's lunacy. Sure, if you looked closely you could see some fuzz and a few black hairs jutting out from Mary's robes and skin, but those would never read on camera.

We had not been told of the liquid starch.

Chiara and I did our best to wring some pungent comedy out of this mess. We filled tape after tape with footage of Lint Lady demonstrating exactly how she collected the lint from her dryer's lint screen. We wanted to re-create the very moment when the inspiration hit to use dryer lint in a craft. In news parody, as the saying goes, when you don't know what else to do, do a reenactment. Reenactments are the first refuge of the lazy, but Chiara and I had to walk away with enough material for a three-minute piece to air on the show in a week's time, and three basic cable minutes are like eight regular minutes.

Again and again we made her scrape the dryer screen and pretend to get this, the most boring of ideas. And each time she did it, we had her vocalize what had gone through her head at the time: the lone word "wow." Her Midwestern timbre and perhaps the acoustics created by the massive wall of her cowl-neck sweater combined to make this "wow" sound just like the braying of a poisoned sheep, or the tattered *bleat, bleat, bleat* of that sheep's now orphaned lamb.

"*Waow.*"

And also like the sound of an old skinny cat whose meow-er has started to break.

"*Waaooowww.*"

Or maybe it was more like the ancient silence of a noble rhesus monkey as it is strapped into its electric shock chair by a faceless, lab-coated researcher for the ten thousandth time. It was so hard to know.

In the awkward stand-around moments while the camera and sound guys wrapped out, Lint Lady's daughter and I picked up a conversation from earlier in the day about our cats. I had described for her my cat, Blanche, who is white with gray spots, and all day long, Lint Daughter had been shifting from foot to foot, dying to show me her cat. "Does your cat look like *this*?" She beamed, producing a white cat with black spots from behind her back. It was a most unmemorable cat, slumped over in the girl's arms, quite annoyed, but the girl was so enamored with it. What I didn't realize then, that I have since realized, is that Blanche might not be memorable to other people, either.

We climbed into our rented Taurus and made off to interview Lint Lady's pastor and try with all our cunning and media might to get him to call her a heretic. I don't think he did.

Oh, and her house overlooked a field where you could see rabbits hopping in the evenings. I remember that, too.

In the final, edited piece, the "wow" moment is milked dry in slow motion, like the venom from a very dull snake. It was all we could do with what we had to work with. Sure, it would be nice if, before you packed up your down-market news parody suit and your eczema medicine and flew thousands of miles to parody reporting a story, some-one actually made sure that something is as linty as it's sup-posed to be, but, like John Lennon said, life just doesn't come with a money-back guarantee.

The same thing happened a few months later in Texas with that Freddie Mercury lady. A researcher at the show had found a woman who claimed she could channel the spirit of Freddie Mercury. Great, we thought, and boarded a plane to Houston. But when the producer and I showed up, the woman, whose name was Petrene, stood at the door, insolently shaking her head. "I'm not talking to Fred-die right now," she said, in that strident tone particular to Australians. "I'm not about to exploit my relationship with him for people's amusement." "Please, please, crazy lady," we cried internally, "you don't understand! We've come here in the *name* of People's Amusement!"

It didn't matter what she had told the researcher on the phone, or that I had flown from Los Angeles, and the pro-ducer had flown from New York, or that we were standing in the Houston steam heat on her porch with a camera guy and a sound guy and appeared for all the world like Dorothy and the Scarecrow and Lion and Tin Man being turned away by the Wizard. (I was Dorothy, the producer was the Scarecrow, and the sound and camera guys could be either the Lion or the Tin Man.) "But we've come such a long way already," I might've said, had I really been carrying out the Dorothy analogy.

After a lot of sweet-talking, Petrene consented to do a little on-camera time traveling for us. She led us into the house, whose every wall was painted a different pastel color and then splattered with a different pastel paint. We'd come to learn during that tedious afternoon that the decor represented the earthly incarnations of the psychic zones that correspond to the Spirit Heart (which we all possess, it turns out) as expressed and filtered by the human mind, and presumably, Wickes Furniture. Not that we were uncomfortable—Petrene's husband kept a constant flow of hot herbal tea at the ready, in case we needed some Mandarin Orange Spice to move more sweat through our pores.

Petrene still refused to call Freddie, so all of our unitards-in-heaven jokes were for naught. All of our fat-bottomed-girls-in-heaven jokes went out the window as well. We tried to work within her approved time-travel parameters, but unfortunately, when Petrene time traveled, it looked a lot like Petrene sitting there, doing nothing. She could be conferring with the Dutch Masters, propelling herself three hundred years into China's future—it didn't matter—she still looked like the same Australian dimwit staring off into space. Now, some amount of dead air for comedic assertion is workable, but too much silence will send your college boys over to FX or SpikeTV in search of some Carl's Jr. commercials to which they can beat off.

The producer wrung his hands and scrambled to make something out of this wretched situation. "Okay, Stace, we can make this work," he said, after some intense reflection and a few short reconnaissance missions around the house. "I've sorted it out with the cameraman. We're gonna make it seem like you go to the bathroom in the future."

I should mention that this man has since been promoted many times.

"This is such a big country," I thought, looking down at the land from thirty thousand feet above. And then, as always, I got the song "In a Big Country" by Big Country stuck in my head. Dammit! This happened nearly every time I flew. Once I got Big Country's "In a Big Country" stuck in my head, I was fucked for a good two hours. Soon after would come the visions of the whole band in their plaid flannel shirts, and that singer (what was his name?) stomping his foot and flopping his eighties mop all over the Scottish Highlands. And then they'd all hop on their Honda ATC's and ride around. If I'm not mistaken, they rode them again in the "Wonderland" video, another song that seemed like it was about the richness and integrity of soil. Was the plaid thing their idea? I wonder. Haircut 100 had their cuddly cable-knit sweaters; Big Country had their earnest plaid. Were pop bands of the eighties coerced to brand themselves with a certain textile? None of it mattered now—for me, it was to be all bagpipes and tartan for the rest of the flight.

A few years ago, I had Yes's "Owner of a Lonely Heart" stuck in my head for a full six months. I don't know how I was chosen or why it visited me for as long as it did, but every morning I'd awake promptly at 11:45 and enjoy a split second of bliss before the sound of synthesizers and samples of breaking glass would fling me out of bed. Then, singer Jon Anderson would start in about moving yourself and proving yourself and the future with his lung-crushing howl.

Long about the third month, I thought, "All right then, this is how it's going to be. This song will be with me for the rest of my life. Everything that happens to me, all of life's coming experiences: an MRI or two, yachting with the boss, grandchildren's birthdays, garden parties, gathering artichokes, burying people, soiling sheets, everything up to the very last hand-holding, Yes's 'Owner of a Lonely Heart' will be right there alongside me."

I suppose it could've been worse. It could've been "Bad to the Bone" or something by the Righteous Brothers.

This was all especially upsetting because I shouldn't have been thinking Scottish at all, I should have been thinking Russian. I was on my way to meet a former Ukrainian pop singer named Aleksandr Prisenchenko who had recently relocated to America and was working as a busboy at a Grand Rapids Best Western Hotel. The intent of the piece was to parody VH1's well-known *Behind the Music* franchise. Our show called it "*Way* Behind the Music." Of course, the first rule of comedy is "Don't Do Some Stupid *VH1 Behind the Music* Parody" (it is an addendum to the "Don't Do an *E! True Hollywood Story* Parody" rule and a precursor to the "Don't Do News Parody" rule, which had yet to be written at this point), but in those days, I didn't ask too many questions, I just gathered my balms and salves and went where they sent me. It's a funny thing, fame. This poor guy was trying to reclaim it, and I was using what I had of it to keep him from doing just that.

The producer Dan and I had worked together about a million times before, but we weren't sure just what to do with Aleksandr. "The basic gist of the story," he had told me on the phone before we each flew out and met in the middle of the country, "is that he was a big star in Russia and now he's a busboy." Dan wasn't asking questions either. We decided the thing to do was to layer the piece with every Russian cliché we could muster to really give it that organic presence that is so vital when it comes to . . . no, that's not it. We just couldn't think of anything else to do. Should we try to make it look like *Dr. Zhivago*? Sure! What's some other Russian-y stuff? Anastasia, Rasputin, *War and Peace*? Okay, that's good. Vodka (pronounced "wodka"), Boris and Natasha, big furry hats, the word *"nyet."* The word *"da."* That's what Russia meant to us, or I should say, that's how Russia "read." Dan was bringing a big furry hat and muff for me to wear in the outdoor shots.

What were they growing down there in those big country fields, anyway? Corn? Soybeans? Rice? Was that hearty patchwork cultivating any of the ingredients present in the delicious Luna bars I never traveled without?

From the makers of Clif Bar, Luna was the bar expressly for women, the bar for *me,* with my discerning taste and all of my pesky, nuanced, fickle, culturally diverse, delicate, empowered, tender, Busy Lady, Having It All needs. For example, one Luna bar provides a full day's worth of dicalcium phosphate *and* magnesium oxide. I don't know about other gals, but if I don't get the recommended daily allowance of dicalcium phosphate *and* magnesium oxide, everyone had better watch it.

Could I afford to indulge in one of my Luna bars right then and there? Let's see, I'd allotted two for the trip out, and I'd already had . . . two. Shit, I'd had Orange Bliss, wherein "the flavors of oranges and cream blend together into one indulgent melody," while waiting to board the first plane, and Nutz Over Chocolate, which put "the scintillating taste of peanuts on a bed of rich dark chocolate," on the way to the airport. I always mapped out my trips in Luna bars—generally rationing two for the trip out, one for a late-night snack in my hotel, two for midshoot snacks, and two to three for the trip home. There are two things I know: in life, there are no money-back guarantees and also, your hotel may not have room service past 10 P.M. Luna bars were my way of taking care of myself, and leaving a little psychological trail by which to find my way back home. The problem always was, once I thought about the bar, I had to have it. It was like they winked at me from the pocket of my carry-on, so much so that I had to secure the bulk of my stash in my suitcase, where I couldn't get to it during the flight. But there was old Tropical Crisp, just inches away in my LeSportSac travel tote. Sweet, sweet Tropical Crisp, so tropical, and so crisp. "Sweet pineapple chunks and a sprinkling of coconut combine for a deliciously sweet and creamy finish," as a matter of fact. If ever a meal replacement bar could have a finish, this one could. I supposed I could spare one little Tropical Crisp.

Besides, I wouldn't *need* three for the trip home. I'd surely find a Cinnabon or an Auntie Anne's Pretzel vendor between now and then. The plan was always to have at least one bar for each leg of the trip, and I knew I'd need one for the prop plane, when the muscles in my face get all scrunched, and my stomach gets so very cold. But no! I unwrapped Tropical Crisp and it was gone in three bites. Goddess wisdom was mine.

I checked into my hotel, a Crowne Plaza. Dan had arrived from New York a few hours earlier, but it was so late that we decided to meet in the morning to go over our plan for the "*Way* Behind the Music," which, I'm positive, will be every bit as fresh with subsequent printings of this book as it was when we shot it on that cold December day at century's end. I took an unfulfilling, too-hot, eczema-inducing bath and then tried to control the damage I had just inflicted on my abraded skin. Eczema sufferers like me had two choices: rub ourselves with cortisone cream, the heroin of topical preparations, which got rid of the problem, but ultimately made it worse by thinning the skin over time, or suffer. I'd suffer as long as I could (aware of the corniness of being in show business with literally thin skin), but I'd inevitably give in.

I put on sleeping clothes, turned on the TV, opened the heavy curtains, closed the heavy curtains, and slithered into bed.

And there it was at 5 A.M.—the crashing of synthesizers (or were they bagpipes?) inside my head. First my alarm went off, and then I got my wake-up call, and then there was the alarm on my cell phone, along with my innate clock that wakes me up every ten minutes, all night long. I don't sleep well in hotels. And I don't ever take chances.

I sat up abruptly in the Crowne Plaza bed, as always, the forest green carpet below me, and the mauve floral-patterned spread pushed aside. Half asleep, I laid out my makeup brushes on the bathroom counter, or technically, the pre-bathroom sink area (the ante-bathroom, I think you call it) and began to brew the in-room complimentary coffee. In the past, I'd plotted how I'd survive in the room were there to be a world-class disaster of some sort. I figured I'd be able to make a crude gruel by mixing the sugar and powdered creamer packets with the drops of tap water that clung to the basin from the night before. I bet I could survive on that for a couple of days if I had to. I could flavor it with some coffee grounds—first the regular, then the decaf. Perhaps I'd even warm it by the light of the desk lamp, if there was electricity.

When I was a kid, we traveled a bit and my older brother and I always shared a room. We'd come in, jump on the beds, take pictures of the toilet, the usual stuff. But as much as I loved vacations and hotels, I'd lie awake at night, my mind racing.

"Cary?" I'd peep after I should've been asleep. "What now?" he'd say. "Cary? Um, if a bad guy broke into this room, he'd get you first, right? Because you've got the bed closest to the door? Right?" There would be some silence and then Cary would answer, "Yeah, I guess." But one night, I think we were in Hawaii, he mulled it over for a while and then answered, "Not if he climbed in the window."

Hotels make me think of things.

With something like TV makeup on, which always looked so shocking at that ungodly hour when I was so alone and so far away from home, I slipped into my shooting outfit. Being from Los Angeles, I have no concept of what my parents call "weather," and being a child of postpunk agony, I am dressed inappropriately for most every situation. Naturally, I never think to have anything like the sort of shoes a person would wear in light snow or the correct inoffensive sweater set that a person wears to interview a small-town mayor. So of course, I was always dressed unsuitably for news parody. Plus, it never gets Michigan cold where I live, so all I had to keep warm was a mildly fortified thin wool jacket. Here it was the dead of winter, and me, without a greatcoat. Great.

"I love to watch your segments and see what clothes you try to get away with," Dan used to say. I did try to conform at first, but somewhere in my second season, I think it was, I grew tired of wearing the One Awful Suit or the Other Awful Suit I had bought expressly to wear on that show, and usually tried to pass something over from my regular, un-news-parody wardrobe. I attempted to supplement my real clothes with some sort of boat-necked casual shirt I'd bought at Banana Republic and returned shortly afterward, but I think it was obvious to anyone who was looking that I wasn't cut out for normal clothes. The standard cornflower blue dress shirt that says "Hello, I'm relatable" has always clashed with my indeterminate skin tone (white with a violet cast, from veins), and I don't want to bust any illusions, but while *The Daily Show with Jon Stewart* may garner all kinds of accolades as America's darling yet caustic lap dog, it does not provide nor reimburse for on-camera clothes. Not even dry cleaning. This is spelled out in the contracts, even: "Artist will not be reimbursed for any dry cleaning costs he may incur." Once, I stepped in a thick pool of mud during a goat story in Lajitas, Texas, and hopelessly marred my Julie-Christie-in-*Don't-Look-Now*-vintage-Ferragamo boots. There was some compulsory chatter of recompense, but I never pursued it.

It didn't really matter what I put on, I was always just try-ing to pass. I'd plan outfits for hours. Could a correspon-dent on, say, *Primetime Live* get away with this top? What if she were one of the younger, hipper types? Or is there just something inherently offensive about it? About me?

During the summer vacation after tenth grade, my friend Missy and I made a real effort to go out and "look for jobs." We hopped into my mom's Celica and drove through Laurel Canyon to Hollywood, like we did every weekend, but this time we walked in and out of every store that sold pointy boots with skull buckles and asked for applications.

That evening, my mother chastised me for going job hunting in a Sid Vicious T-shirt, pointy boots with buckles, ripped black tights, and a fringed micro-miniskirt that was really just a long shirt with the top cut off at the waist. "What?" I thought. "What's wrong with what I'm wearing?" It's not like my boots had the skull buckles or anything.

"You can't go out looking for a job like that," she scolded. "Even your friend knew enough to wear a little dress."

Indeed, Missy had worn a little dress, and its fabric design was of spiders and spiderwebs. Why was that okay?

Even when I did try in earnest to come close to a news getup, things never fit right. They tugged and pulled in weird places. And the combination of air travel, unfamiliar climates, and too many Luna bars made my limbs swell like gourmet pretzel dough.

I made my way out to the Crowne Plaza dining room, makeup blaring, notes under arm, pulling my olive green suitcase behind me. It was still dark out. I sat alone, waiting for Dan and thinking, "How can this be? It's 9 A.M., isn't it? Is my watch wrong? Is my cell phone clock wrong? Was the in-room clock wrong (because that had happened to me before)? Also, was the wake-up call wrong? Where is the sun?"

Other guests sat in the dining room, reading *USA Today* like nothing was wrong. I ordered pancakes and coffee and a small orange juice that tasted of tin. Still no Dan, still no light. Michigan is north, but it's not Helsinki. It was 9:25 and still no change. Maybe Grand Rapids is the Land of the 9 A.M. Midnight. At 9:27, Dan stumbled into the dining room. "Sorry!" he said.

"Dan, it's pitch black outside! Where are we?" I whined. He looked out the window. "Huh," he said, and nothing more.

We each pulled out our legal pads and went over our interview questions. First, there were the general, get-these-out-of-the-way-and-make-it-seem-like-we-actually-want-to-know-the-answers questions: Where are you from? Can you describe your music for me? What are your goals? How are you enjoying America, Alex? I always kept a few of these benign inquiries up my (figurative or literal) Awful Suit Sleeve for when I needed to grease and distract my subject. If ever an interviewee started to get hip to the fact that I was, say, making him look, oh, I don't know, foolish for, say, inventing a pair of flatulence filtering pants, or whatever he was doing, I'd always look at him naively and begin to guide the conversation in another direction until I could end up at, "So, how are you liking fall here in Aberdeen?" or something along those lines. Not that we were there to mock, or gawk—that's for schoolyard bullies. In media, there are no mean spirits. "Mean-spirited" is a phrase that will get you a chorus of scowls. It's a phrase that triggers everyone around the conference table to shake his head and rumble, "No, no, we don't want that. That's not what we're about." In media, we don't make fun, we celebrate. We want to *celebrate the eccentricities* of these people, our beloved subjects, our adorable little gnat brains.

Dan and I were about to celebrate the fuck out of old Alex P. from Ukraine. He'd be invited to the party, too, of course—able to partake of the passed appetizers and the open bar (until 10 P.M.), but the difference was, Dan and I and our buddy the editor would still be celebrating long after Alex had said good night and gone up to bed. Weeks later, in the edit bay, during voiceovers, sound effects, music cues, the festivities would still be limping along. We were the friend who stays at the party until dawn, pouring the backwashed ends of beers together trying to make one last whole beer.

My nausea set in with the rising sun during the rental-car ride to Alex's house. The night before I had plied myself with lots of sleep-inducing herbs: valerian root, Rescue

Remedy, kava kava, melatonin, BeWell, Calmy Calm-Calm, Nicethoughts, Happysafeyou, and whatever other standardized extracts, pellets, and tinctures I'd gotten at my neighborhood health food store. My hotel room looked like the aftermath of a weird holistic party—as if Jack LaLanne had come round with some whores and laid out lines of brewer's yeast and we all stayed up really late. I could see in the passenger-side mirror that my makeup was already molting and tarnishing the way it does when I've tried too hard. Additionally, those coarse hotel sheets always aggravated my eczema, causing red blotches to surface across jaw, upper lip, chin, and throat in their all too familiar U.S. Virgin Islands pattern. I wonder if there is a special branch of housekeeping staff, maybe trafficked humans, that never comes outside, that stays down in the dank, peeling bowels of the hotel, stirring and stirring white sheets and towels into huge metal vats of bleach. One can never be certain what happens in the bottoms of big buildings. At one point I started traveling with my own soft, good-smelling pillowcase from home until I realized that kind of thing made me a weirdo.

I don't suspect this kind of discomfort is much of a problem for Crowne Plaza guests anymore, ever since the Crowne Plaza Sleep Advantage Program. Did I forget to mention that these were the days before the Crowne Plaza Sleep Advantage Program? It seems unbelievable now, but the Crowne Plaza didn't always offer Lavender Sleep Spray or the Heavenly Bed, or the Eye Pillow, or any of those things. Back in the late nineties, all they gave you was the bleached-out sheets, the mauve floral spread, and a weird blanket with stiff, short synthetic fur like a mole's, but beige. The blanket was about the farthest thing from restful or welcoming, and gave the impression that it shouldn't be allowed to touch your bare skin. It was an altogether antiseptic piece of bulk bed linen that made me question, Has there ever been a beige mole, like an albino mole? It wouldn't make the least bit of biological sense, seeing as how moles are nocturnal and only operate underground. Come to think of it, I've never actually seen a mole, and, come to think of it, I don't think I've even seen a nature documentary on moles. I know I've never gone to the library and checked out a book about moles. Yet, I know a little about moles. How can people like me know about moles if they're not even on TV? Things *have* to be on TV.

But what if there were such a mole—an albino mole? Would his absence of pigment be an advantage, or a liability? Wouldn't a mole want to be seen by all the other moles in his community? How can he hope to gain their admiration? Would the other moles kill him for being different, or would they revere him like a god? I think they would revere him for a while, and then kill him when they got tired of him.

Alex P. opened the door and invited us into his tidy little home. His hair had the hazy-film look milk chocolate gets when it's left in a drawer for over a year, but by contrast, his face was the booming, rosy face of Eastern Europe, always squinting itself into a big smile.

The Prisenchenko home looked to be made out of remnants of other houses, and then covered in siding. Nothing looked straight or level, as if all the rooms had been pushed together by a slow-moving stream that later dried up. The floor was a patchwork of dark, brawny carpets: royal blue to kelly green. There was a standard kitchen, garnished with grease-sheened ruffles and powder blue potholders with tiny hearts. Here and there were hung painted tiles, illustrations of eggplants, mushrooms, gourds. On the counter was a tin of authentic old-fashioned cocoa mix from a warehouse club store. I checked my makeup in the light of the tidy bathroom and for one second considered scrubbing my face bare with the Dial liquid soap and then raking it back and forth on the furry old toilet seat cover. But instead, I exited the bathroom and calmly took a seat on the living room couch. I fixed my eyes on the framed pictures on the walls. They were of humans, in situations: kids playing in those bouncy-ball chambers, someone sitting on a pony somewhere, an old, old lady when she was younger, a frilly bridal party under a gazebo.

I chatted with Alex's wife about Michigan. My mother came from around here. I had family south of here somewhere. I'd been swimming in the lake with its tiny, tiny waves.

The camera and sound guys had faced two wooden dining chairs embarrassingly close together for our interview. Alex and I "sat in," as they say in TV, and he started to tell me things right away. Things about Ukraine, and his busboy job at the Best Western, and how he liked music that "is having lots of garmony." I wanted to ask him if he'd like to teach the world to sing in perfect garmony, but I didn't feel it was all that funny, and besides, the camera wasn't on yet.

"So, tell me, Alex, how are you liking Grand Rapids?"

He smiled and told me he liked it very much. He chose to settle here "because weather being like Ukraine." Of course, I say, Ukrainians always say they miss the weather most.

So, when did I get so mean? It's impossible to say, but four situations come to mind that certainly didn't help.

I had a friend in elementary school named Diana Kittay who had simple tastes: she liked TV westerns, playing dress-up with floppy hats, and drawing bunnies. I called her "Diana Kitty Litter," of course. Who wouldn't? It was the most natural of progressions: winter turns to spring, a young man grows old, "Kittay" becomes "Kitty Litter" in the child mind. The whole matter was of little consequence to her or anyone else.

One day, as I bounded up Diana's steps with my little play bag with its apple design and the words "I Like You," I called out, "Hey, Kitty Litter!" I said, "Am I too late for *Big Valley*?"

"Um, my mom says you shouldn't say that anymore," said Diana.

"*Big Valley*?"

"No, Kitty Litter. She says that's not our name and it's rude."

Really? The thrust of it unsnapped itself like a blackjack into my guts. It wasn't even something I had been that proud of. I hadn't even been trying. If I had been trying to offend you, Mrs. Kittay, bitch, you'd know.

That was one thing.

After not landing a job in any skull-buckle-boot shops, I

spent my sixteenth summer as something called a "show controller" at Universal Studios Theme Park just near Hollywood. I was made to wear a pair of gender-impartial, roomy-fit, eggshell-colored chinos with a striped canvas belt and an Agreeable Red Short-Sleeved Shirt with hokey white buttons and a name tag. At this time, I was wearing my hair hacked short by a pink Daisy shaver and my yarn-dry ends told many coppery tales of improperly used bleach. I have rarely been uglier than I was that summer.

My job was to get tourists in and out of the park attractions swiftly and painlessly. If the Conan the Barbarian show was at capacity, I'd have to draw the arena's heavy black curtain, close the barbaric doors, and inform the crowds through my megaphone that "the four-thirty Conan the Barbarian show is full. It's FULL. *F-U-L-L.*"

And oh, the lies people would tell to get into the four-thirty Conan the Barbarian show. "But my wife/brother/husband/mail-order bride/father-in-law/pastor/facialist/oxygen tank is in there! I have to get in!" It was up to me to decide whose concerns were valid and warranted a mid-show escort to a seat. Invariably, I'd determine that no one was worth a possible reprimand from the stage actors.

Later, I'd meet the same bunch of cocks over at the stunt show, a Western-themed act performed by real Hollywood ex-stuntmen and based around a narrative about betrayal, gunslinging, good, evil, and whisky. I'd have to scrape closed the heavy wooden doors to the stunt fortress while hearing the same excuses and the same bullshit.

Then I'd meet these very same slags again over at the park's biggest draw. I can't remember the show's name, but it was something like the "Let's See How Movies Are Made with Movie Magic" show, where the lucky few were selected from the audience to come onstage and participate in real live simulations of movie magic. Some dopey family got to put on rip-away costumes and take pies in the face in front of a green screen and then everyone watched it all put together with movie magic as a movie. This is where I learned that there are people among us who would bruise my soft white limbs on the minute chance that they might catch a glimpse of themselves pretending to jump over a building in a Keystone Kop getup. And that's a hard truth to swallow.

Back at school and still twitching from my ugly-human summer, I developed a friendship with a girl named Jennifer Perrine (rhymes with "terrine").

One afternoon at Jennifer's house, which was nestled even more snugly in a vine-ripened nook of the Sherman Oaks hills than my own, Jennifer and I worked on our creative writing homework while her mother steamed dinner in a bamboo basket in the kitchen. Her mother was from China; her father was a Dutch guy. Jennifer and her sister didn't need to shave their legs.

We were waist high in a unit on the descriptive sentence. Miss Rampandahl, who looked like Eileen Brennan in *Private Benjamin* and whom Jennifer called Miss Rabiddog, had had us pruning and polishing our one sentence for nigh on three weeks now. Every time the class turned in its revised sentences, Rabiddog would hand the sentences back the next day with little green marks indicating where we missed opportunities to add description. She distributed lists that we pored over the whole period: all the ways to say something is yellow, or blue, or sharp, or cloudy. My sentence was about bacon frying. What more could I describe other than the twisted, gnarled, knotted, knobby, greasy, oily, slimy clots of clotty, hazy knots of grizzled cloudy foggy fat that bulged and spurted and cackled as the moist muscle shrunk into scaly russet waves within the oilyhotness of the pan, black and dangerous as fresh tar? I knew 'ddog would have something to say about the unexamined choice of the words "black" and "hot," and I thought she might not go for "oilyhotness" but I found the unexpected subtlety of "black" to be refreshing, and as for "oilyhotness," well, I'd like to hear Rabiddog tell e.e. cummings that "mudlucious" is not a word.

I really would, I would like to hear that.

Jennifer was on her ninth draft of a sentence about the stiffness, crispness, and fullness of Bono's onyx-colored jeans when her mother bobbed her head in the door.

"Girls, *bao*."

Jennifer shrugged her brown shoulders and her pink bunny mouth darted sideways into a bit of a sneer. "She just came back from China again."

We sat at the enormous driftwood coffee table while Mrs. Perrine ladled a gooey, cloudy, steamy, soft, pale orb of glutinous rice gush onto each black plate. Jann, the Perrine family friend with the hand-knit tunic and the spiffy little beard, came in from the kitchen.

"You girls are in for a treat. May Lee makes excellent *bao*."

"It ought to be good, I brought the flour back with me from Taipei," said Jennifer's mother, folding her little world-weary legs underneath her on the cold, lapis lazuli–colored tile floor that looked like what I thought rivers in China must look like. *The Joy Luck Club* was still a few years off, but already I was imagining blue, deep, glossy bodies of water, older than even the ancestors, flowing through villages like the music from a Chinese kind of flute, giving life to life-giving rice flour, worked by a legacy of hands.

But it tasted like shit. I stabbed at the *bao* with my lacquered chopstick, feeling, above all, abandoned. The bland thing was filled with stringy shredded pork. The only pork I liked was bacon pork. Not actual pig pork.

May Lee leafed through *Sunset* magazine, chewing her *bao* and humming to herself what was maybe a Mandarin wedding hymn, or the theme to *St. Elsewhere*. And I was stuck in an emblematic problem of my youth: How best to discard of the gross, other-family food?

I tried to catch Jennifer's eye, but her mind was deep in Bono's pockets again. I figured I'd eat just the dough part, longing all the while for some kind of sauce, but I'd never dare ask for sauce. I wasn't that kind of kid. I'm not that kind of adult. My friend Leisel, on the other hand, is a classic sauce-asker. "They're good," she once said of the crepes at a French restaurant we both like, "but that place won't give you any Tabasco."

As luck would have it, Jann wandered back through the room and started a conversation with May Lee, something about gardening and Isabella Rossellini—standard mid-eighties chatter.

"Jennifer," I whispered. "Do you want the rest of mine?" She didn't hear me.

"You know in Vermont we'd use our coffee grounds as mulch," Jann said.

"Oh, what a good idea!" said May Lee.

"Hey, Purina Cat Chow," I said, trying to time my words to their mulch talk. Jennifer finally heard me, but so did May Lee. She whipped her head around, and a tide of distress rose in her throat.

Jennifer Purina Cat Chow. Yes, I called her that. No, not all the time, but sometimes, when the mood hit me. Jennifer didn't mind.

"Well, I don't think it very nice name to call someone," said May Lee, probably without the demeaning little parlance I'm assigning her now.

Really, these puns, if you could even call them that, were by no means my best work. I would go on, in life, to do much more impacting compositions—to write three-minute *Erin Brockovich* parodies starring Kirsten Dunst and Jimmy Fallon, and that's just to start, but for what they were, "Kittay Litter" and "Cat Chow" were adequate, harmless nicknames that even had a nice, accidental feline symmetry, not that anyone cared.

I used to live with a recreational actress named Agnes who passed most of her days hunched over in her room talking on the phone, drinking thick, tart coffee, smoking, and tugging at her hair, deep in thought. She'd grasp at each clump of hair with her index and middle fingers, and then roll the pad of her thumb all over the ends. She had a massive scar across her face from a trolley accident, but she was

185

nice. Her big cool friend was a well-known casting director who always "wanted to" cast her in things, but never did. He'd breeze into town and Aggie would be all atwitter. Inevitably, the casting friend would give her a few days' work as his casting assistant. He'd let her read for whatever part they were casting, and she'd never get it. "No one gets me!" she'd croak, the massive scar across her face seeming to pulse with poison. If only she could've milked it like they do with snakes, into a cup.

Agnes was just one of the many Ungotten. I know, I've felt that way, too.

No one *gets* me! No one *gets* me!

Least of all the two of you, Mrs. Kittay and Perrine, bonded together by your mutual revulsion at the notion of someone making a wordplay out of your names. Your precious names. Tell me, ladies, what's it like to be so conventional? Does it feel good? Do you feel justified? Say, Mrs. Kitty Litter, didn't I see you adrift in the theme park crowd? Yes, I believe I heard you lying about an oxygen tank as you crushed my ribs against the massive doors while the Eternal Stuntman held your hoodie and snickered. And wasn't it you, Purina Cat Chow, standing center stage, pulling on a Keystone Kop uniform, turning your head to meet the coming whipped cream pie, as the rash that lay dormant under my skin began to exert its familiar U.S. Virgin Islands pattern across my scowling face?

"It is difficult to make and find job about music," Alex told me when I asked him about his new life in America.

"Even here, in Grand Rapids, the music capital of the world?" I asked, as earnestly as possible.

"Yes, even here."

This interview was dying, and it was only the beginning of the shoot. The plan was to first do a sit-down interview with Alex and then one with his wife, Mary Anne Bohatch. That was her name. Then, Alex would sing us a song from his new CD, titled *Gift to a Friend to the Year 2000*. After that, we'd repair to the Best Western, shoot some miscellaneous stuff, and reveal the big reveal: that Alex worked there as a busboy. Funny, right?

I asked him about his musical influences. He said he much liked the Beatles and "Ja Cocker." I was growing more and more bored.

"Tell me about Typhoon," I demanded. Alex perked up at the mention of his old band.

"Yes, young people are very like it my group company, my group Typhoon." He told of adoring fans and sparkly shirts, of record company dinners, of shrimp cocktail, of pale wine in crystal goblets, and chocolate mousse for dessert.

"It is like, eh, chocolate cup of air. You are knowing this sweets?"

I was knowing this sweets, all right.

Alex told tales of—well, to be honest, I was barely listening. I was, like all good parody journalists, planning what I was going to say next, when the sight of Alex's young son watching us from his little plastic car thing caught my eye. It was one of those bulbous, brightly colored Fisher-Price-looking things that I sometimes see turned over in people's yards and think, "God, I never want one of those turned over in my yard."

"Can? Can? Where is Can?" chirped Alex, looking around. We were all a bit confused. Why did he want a can?

"Oh, there are you," he said, looking past the camera. "Can, you are going to putting photo of Typhoon into camera?"

"Oh," answered Dan. "Yes, of course, we'll shoot the Typhoon photos later, after the interview."

I thought it time to ask Alex my final question, which had been prepared in advance, in Russian.

"Vidja nite ey Yakova Smirnova? Ochen smish noya, da?"

Alex laughed and answered in Russian that yes, he did know this Yakov Smirnoff, and he is very funny, yes.

That's right, friends, it had come to Yakoff Smirnoff references. I may as well have fried some ants with a magnifying glass while I was at it. For some reason, although he was and is wealthier and more famous than Alex and me put together, Yakoff Smirnoff represents something that we could both safely look down on. I don't know just what causes that.

Next up was the wife. Mary Anne Bohatch was an American woman who was somewhat of a fixture in the former Soviet Union pop scene. Fair enough. During our interview, she told me how she met Alex at a Typhoon show. He had spotted her in the crowd and made arrangements with his guy to have her brought backstage.

Coincidentally, this had been the fantasy I'd based the first thirty years of my life on: I will be spotted in the crowd and ushered into a superior life. This was not ironic joke fodder, this was real, but in my situation, here, on very little sleep, tin orange juice, no Lavender Sleep Spray, and a television show depending on me, I had to put my personal feelings aside and do what I had been flown here coach to do: I made Mrs. Prisenchenko come off like a common groupie while her husband and son smiled nearby, oblivious. Whether or not she had technically been a groupie, Mary Anne had no idea what I was up to, so it was okay.

It was finally time to hear Alex sing. He offered to perform anything off the new CD. Dan and I scanned the titles. "My Hard Life," "I Wasted My Young Years," "Don't Grieve," and "My Songs Are Crying" all sounded tempting, but we chose to hear the simply titled "Sorry."

Alex accompanied himself on acoustic guitar and sang with the loudest voice I have ever heard. "Sorry" was in Russian, but the lyrics translated to something about killing his broken heart with a tall stick. The little boy looked so enraptured as his father sang you'd think he was watching Raffi himself.

I wonder as I write this how many future narrative non-fiction essays I will make an appearance in. Will *Best New Narrative Nonfiction Voices, 2024* have essays with titles like "The Lady Who Made Fun of Dad" and "They Said They Were From Television"? Will the little kids on plastic car-things grow up, place fingers to keypads, and write things like "I thought she looked so nice in her relatable corn-flower blue dress shirt, but something seemed sinister about her, like how she was always looking at herself in that compact mirror, and the way she left so quickly. She didn't even say good-bye"?

Outside the Grand Rapids Best Western is where we shot the B-roll of Alex and me walking and pretending to have a conversation. I wore the big furry hat and muff and strolled along as if I were in St. Petersburg.

"Sometimes I see dream, my dream," said Alex, not realizing (or caring?) that he wasn't miked because this part was to have no sound. "One dream I speak together. I sit down Paul McCartney. I sit down this. I speak to Paul McCartney. Why?"

(I hadn't asked why.)

"I don't know. But I believe dream. Dream is correct information to give from life."

True as this was, we had enough footage now, and besides, Alex's shift started in a few minutes.

"Maybe sometimes I will here popular," he said, mostly to the snow.

While Alex got to the business of busing tables in the dining room, the crew set up to interview the Best Western's food service manager in the adjacent Bar Tropicale. I found a bathroom and checked my hair. There was no telling what damage the big furry hat might have done to it.

The changing table in the ladies' room looked so inviting, I had to lay down a few paper towels and rest my head on it, just for a second or two.

A few years earlier I had read all but the last twenty pages of *Crime and Punishment*. As the coolness of the pink Formica counter penetrated my cheekbone, I wondered what Raskolnikov would have thought of Grand Rapids. Would he have wandered the avenues in too light a coat because he had to sell his greatcoat for some mozzarella sticks from Applebee's to keep from starving? Would he finally decide to rob and kill an insignificant person, like he had the old lady pawnbroker back in St. Petersburg, in order to survive? Would he justify it by telling himself that no one would miss her and he didn't get caught so it wasn't really a crime? And if so, how long would he be haunted by the guilt? How long would I? If an insignificant Ukrainian pop singer falls in a buffet restaurant of a discount hotel chain in Michigan, does it make a sound? What if it's on basic cable, as part of a *VH1 Behind the Music* parody? No one will mourn Aleksandr Prisenchenko, will they? *Ochen smish noya, da?*

Maybe in the last twenty pages Raskolnikov does get caught and is made to pay for his crime. I should really finish it.

We crossed the dining room on our way into the bar and I caught a glimpse of the Best Western buffet where Dan had unthinkingly arranged for our lunch break to take place. There were rows of ambiguous salads, fruit cocktails, tumbling gelatin peaks, and pudding blends. Everything was certainly from a large can stored somewhere in the bowels of the hotel. Alex was patiently helping an old woman get just the right mix of ambrosia from the buffet. She seemed not to want certain cuts of cherry.

The Bar Tropicale was different from the dining room. It had a bar and a mural on one wall. Set against a standard island backdrop was painted a lone cockatoo that sat face-to-face with a soft, weightless daiquiri. They were each so far from home. Did they sometimes talk to pass the lonely hours? I'll bet the daiquiri just sat there in silence, while the cockatoo longed for a chance to mimic it. I'll bet this is happening still.

I conducted a quick and painful interview with the food service manager, Henry Bouthiette, a squirrelly-looking man with a dishwater blond mustache and a Hawaiian shirt. I'm sorry to say it went exactly like this:

STACEY: What do you think of Aleksandr as an artist?

HENRY BOUTHIETTE: I don't know, I haven't heard his music.

STACEY (artificial shock): But you're his manager!

HENRY BOUTHIETTE: I don't manage him in the music business, I manage him in the restaurant business.

Booiinnggg!

You could almost feel the wind from that arrow as it shot into the center of the bull's-eye. He's a busboy! The *Behind the Music* parody punch line we've been building to this whole time? Alex's big comeback—is as a busboy!

That joke was seen not just coming down the block— that joke was seen getting up, getting in a town car, taking three flights (all coach) and a cab to its hotel and once there, checking its e-mail, watching *Law & Order,* taking a bath, falling asleep, waking early, putting on a cornflower blue dress shirt, taking three trips in a rental car, coming in, sitting down, checking its makeup, breathing an inaudible sigh, and laying itself out. And the payoff? The payoff was as sweet and rare as an industrial-sized can of Del Monte fruit cocktail.

We used our lunch break as an opportunity to shoot

some B-roll of Alex in action. It was at this time that Dan and I got it: the worst of all ideas.

We've all seen someone at a restaurant indicate that they want more coffee by doing a condescending little point-at-cup-with-tentative-half-smile thing. "Well," we thought (all right, *I* thought), "why not do that to Alex?"

"Oh, we can't! That is so wrong!" and we laughed the laugh that basic cable talent and producers laugh when they think something is funny.

"It's so wrong!" he said.

"I know, it's *so wrong!*" I said.

But the thing was, once Dan and I started laughing about something, it was too late. We had behaved on many occasions like obnoxious little jerks, unable to stifle our giggles for even one clean take. The mere mention of the word "diarrhea" was enough to set the production schedule back a good eight minutes, and "masturbating with diarrhea" would add a couple of minutes to that. There is no way to explain this without sounding like an ass, but it's a bit late for that now, anyway.

We got me a cup of coffee and filled a plate with the foods from the buffet that we thought would read funniest: fluffy, pastel-colored things, like ambrosia, cheese cubes, and what looked to be a nondairy-whipped-topping-based chocolate "mousse," which was certainly forever mocking poor Alex. Was it hard to have to clear away plates with remnants of uneaten mousse on them? And every night, when he scraped what was left in the buffet bowl into the trash and each morning cranked open a new can from the storeroom, what was going through his mind?

Maybe he thought, "What a country!"

Up until now, the Best Western had literally been the best that the Western world had to offer Aleksandr Prisenchenko. He had been working hard, direct-depositing his checks, dreaming of Tuesdays with Sir Paul, and biding his time until the day a television show would finally spot him in the crowd and escort him past the ropes. That's how America "read" to him.

When in fact, that's exactly how it had happened to me. A year earlier, I was sleeping one late morning in my Fairfax District apartment, for which rent was due and not yet foreseeable, when the phone rang.

"Stacey? You're a hard woman to track down!" said the phone. "This is Carrie Blahblahson from Chris Soandso's office at Comedy Central. We'd like you to be on our TV show called *The Daily Show*. Would you like to be on our TV show?"

I had seen it. I liked it. I said I would.

"Well, that's a lucky break," I thought, heading back to bed. Now I could stop all this worrying about my future.

Alex saw my plate and warned me not to eat too much— he was making us a very special Russian dinner tonight that we were going to love. We hadn't planned on going back to his place after the shoot, but Dan and I got the impression that it would break his heart if we didn't, and we didn't want to break his heart—any more than we needed to.

With the camera back on, I pretended to eat my ambrosia and when Alex bustled by, I held up my coffee cup and did the little passive-aggressive, hopeful, faux-meek pantomime we had planned.

We expected him to have some combination of the following reactions:

Laugh off the request.

Do it, but somehow indicate through humor that he's playing along.

Become indignant.

Become indignant and storm out, saying, "Excuse me, but I'm not the production assistant on this."

Pull someone aside and say, "Hi, um, this is supposed to be a piece on me and my singing, and I don't think it looks good for me to be serving you, do you see where I'm coming from?"

That's what *we* would've done. A hip TV show comic actress from Hollywood and her gay New York producer; we had grown accustomed to just enough luxury to be dangerous. We would've made some phone calls, gone and smoked defiantly in the corner, demanded to be alone for a while and eventually talked down. We expected any version of those things from Alex, but we could've never predicted what he actually did: he smiled, said, "Sure," and got me more coffee.

It is only now that I am beginning to understand his reaction. Alex comes from a place, though I know not if it's physical or metaphorical, where people give you coffee when you would like coffee. What happens is this: a person is having some coffee and then wants more coffee, and, for whatever reason, the person who is the one to provide the coffee in the scenario gives him or her more of the coffee he or she desires. And that's it. It has nothing to do with status, or television, or love. You don't take it to the grave, it doesn't lie dormant like a rash under your skin, it isn't one of your *Artist's Way* journaling exercises, it doesn't inspire a one-woman show, and you don't work through your feelings about it in Group. All it is is this: coffee is needed, coffee is given.

We needed to pick up some stand-ups here and there—those shots that always show the correspondent strolling in front of something representative of the area and saying, "But here in [city], one man is [fighting back or hoping to change all that or, in the case of our show, building a welcome station for the aliens]." We still thought we might come up with some great bit that would save this piece. Alex wiped his hands on his apron and made us promise to come back to his place when we were done for the special meal he'd been planning for the last two weeks.

Oh, shit.

For the rest of the day, we scavenged in the snow, turning over rocks and logs, hoping to find some great swarm of jokes underneath. Hello? Anything funny under here? We dipped our sticks into tree holes, hopeful that when we pulled them out they'd be teeming with satisfying ants, but no such luck. The snow and the wind kicked up and the sky darkened, so we called it a wrap and went back to Alex's.

When we arrived, the table was set with a lace cloth, china, and goblets filled with ice water. There were candles in candlesticks, and Mary Anne Bohatch had changed into a dress.

Alex was like an expectant father, dashing around, mumbling, wringing his hands, tugging at his apron. He seated us quickly and Dan, Mary Anne, the kid, and I sipped water and smiled shyly at each other.

"Have you ever had Russian food?" asked Mary Anne.

I started to relay a cool anecdote about borscht, when a timer went off.

"Oooo," said Mary Anne. Dan simultaneously said "ooo."

Alex entered from the kitchen with a tray and placed on each of our plates one steaming-hot microwaved Chicken Kiev Hot Pocket.

"Can you believe?" he beamed. "They make this way— so easy now! It is this country and mine together! It is world of best boths!"

Sometimes, if you listen very closely, the wind can sound just like a cat with a broken meow-er.

Invented in 1995, Hot Pockets, like the entire range of sandwiches that make up the order of "handheld foods," consist of two or more fillings, generally within a theme, that are wrapped inside a flaky, bakery-style crust. In China, they're called *bao*.

Handhelds were indeed a breakthrough: until 1995, a dish like chicken Kiev had to be eaten with at least one fork.

The Hot Pocket is also an emblem of comedic hackery. In comedy circles, it is better to say nothing and be thought a fool than to make a Hot Pocket reference.

I thought I could sort of gnaw at the bakery-style crust and drizzle the Kiev around on the plate in such a way that might disguise how little I'd be eating. Unfortunately, Dan was doing the same thing. And the Prisenchenkos noticed.

Dan and I knew what we had to do. You can come to his house, you can laugh at his dreams, but you should never, ever disrespect a man's Pocket.

We ate furiously and silently. The Prisenchenkos followed our lead. Before I knew it, there was another Pocket on each of our plates. We ate and ate, Pocket upon Pocket. The microwave was on constant hum. Alex said something in Russian (or was it English?) about all of our healthy appetites. I think that's what he said, but he needn't have said anything. You don't need words when you both speak fluent Hunger. Partially hydrogenated palm oil drooled invisibly out the corners of my mouth, investing itself into my cells to make marionette lines of blemish in the ensuing weeks. These pockets, so handy, so contrived, were just holders of sorrow—papooses of longing, filling one up with rubber and flake until one must feed again, for fame is a hunger that cannot be appeased by any Pocket, by some mock French dessert, anything at the earthly buffet. We're not so different, Alex and I. I even have the same dream, except in mine it's Ringo, but that's unimportant. Alex and I have the same master, I'm just the house nigger, is all, and I'm all too happy to sell out the ones in the field to stay in good with whitey. To sleep in the bigger house, with the better sheets. I'm an informant, really. I'm the mole.

So why was I here?

It may have something to do with the fourth thing.

In 1989, before I worked at a little record store on Melrose in Hollywood, I worked in a little record store on Ventura Boulevard in Sherman Oaks. It was just me and the assistant manager, Brent, a quiet little guy whom I'd gone to elementary school with. His twin brother, Brad, was well known for the homespun tattoo of the cover of Pink Floyd's *Dark Side of the Moon* that he had on his arm. Brent was kind, had long hair, and could draw well. He had a dog named Stovepipe, and he loved the band Marillion very, very much.

It was almost time to close, and there was the usual gaggle of lonely men still scouring the used record bins for anything they might have overlooked and arranging and rearranging their stacks of Manassas and Robin Trower records, or whatever they had that night. A tall, elderly man walked through the front door shouting and waving a gun around. He made all the customers get into one corner of the store and he told me to open up the register. I gave him all that was there, which wasn't much.

Then, he took Brent and me into the back room to open the safe. Brent was just recently made assistant manager and had only opened the safe a handful of times. His fingers failed try after try. The man held the gun on me and told Brent he'd better get that fucking safe open on three.

Brent's artistic little fingers shook harder as he tried to do the combination again. The bathroom door was open, and I couldn't help but glance at the mirror. I might see myself die. I saw my face, as white as paper, and I saw the gun. Behind me I could see all the customers over in the corner, where they had been herded. Their heads were bent down, and they were shopping. Still sifting through the record bins. There might be some rare find in the corner, and they just couldn't help but indulge.

Brent unlocked the safe right on three, and the man took the money and ran out the back door into the alley.

"Are you guys okay?" asked exactly one of the customers when Brent and I came back into the store. Brent quickly got on the phone to the police, and the guys lined up at the counter in front of me.

I just stared at them. What did they want?

"Can I pay for this?" one of them asked, setting a twenty-nine-cent record next to the register. I think it was by Ambrosia.

I didn't know how to react, so I said nothing and rang it up. The rest of the customers followed suit. I rang them up, too. I didn't yet know about smoking defiantly in the corner, and there was no one to pull aside and say, "Hi, um, you just saw me with a gun at my head, right? Well, if you made me ring up your records now, it might look kind of bad, like, my life doesn't matter at all. Do you see what I'm saying?"

The first question people always ask about *The Daily Show with Jon Stewart* (after "Is Jon Stewart nice? Because he seems like he'd be really nice") is "When you do those interviews, how do you keep a straight face?" I usually say something about the mood being very serious when you're in the situation. I say that because to explain that I see each one of them shoving, or reprimanding, or demanding Ambrosia would take too long to explain. And it would probably make me sound like a weirdo.

My shirt was fitting so, so badly on the flights home. There wasn't any need to load up on Auntie Anne's pretzels or even stop at the candy and nuts wagon. The Chicken Kiev Hot Pockets would be amending themselves inside me for hours to come. All I had was a *Vanity Fair* to help while away the hours. I rubbed the new Burberry fragrance on my wrist and read about a party at some palazzo in Venice that was attended by members of the Belgian aristocracy.

Two weeks later, "*Way* Behind the Music: Aleksandr Prisenchenko" premiered. The in-studio response was dim. You couldn't necessarily hear crickets so much as one disappointed cricket, who sort of half chirped and then made some excuse about having to get up early before slipping out. Not even the furry hat made much of an impact, and we were so sure the furry hat would *kill*.

Alex called the office the next day and told Dan how much he and Mary Anne had liked the piece, how funny it was, and how good it had been to meet us. This is something I'll never understand. The only explanation I have is that ultimately, people just want to be on TV. I should know—I'm people. Oh, I'm people, all right.

A year later, the singer of Big Country was found swinging by the neck from a rope in a hotel room in Hawaii.

Most shocking to me was the fact that Big Country had been consistently putting out records all this time. There had been at least ten post-plaid releases. I can't imagine they were still in plaid. Certainly at some point, a decision had to have been made to abandon the plaid. I'm sure the members of Big Country justified it thusly: "Look, we did what we had to do to get noticed, to give people something to identify with, but we want to move beyond that now." But they never really did. Move beyond that. Still, I guess everyone has to wear the shirt of compromise sometimes, just in case.

As the song goes, "In a big country, dreams stay with you," and I guess they stayed with him all the way to Hawaii. They also, according to the song, enable you to "live and breathe and see the sun in wintertime." He saw the sun in wintertime, unlike me. In that Crowne Plaza breakfast room, and in all the breakfast rooms hence, all I saw was darkness.

I've been doing this long enough that some of my former interviewees have actually died. There was poor old Carmine Spagnolia, with his blackheads the size of houseflies—he didn't have long, we all knew it. And there was the teenage girl whose mother I had spoken with at great length about the lone spatula she was selling in the classified ads. What she must have thought of me. The girl was on house arrest, and I found out recently that her body had been discovered near a Dumpster in a rival gang's territory. There was a misunderstanding of some sort, I was told. And then there was the old man who changed his name to "God" and slept in a metal pyramid. He was found hanging in his little Hollywood apartment. And I'm sure there are others I don't know about: old Terry Johnson who lived in a cluttered office in Long Beach, drawing picture after picture depicting the anal sex he was forced to have with celebrities every night aboard that spaceship. And what about the man in the Las Vegas trailer who cooks down all his mucus and saves it in labeled Mason jars? Could he, now as I'm writing and now again as you're reading, still be doing that? Standing dutifully over the little range plate, burning, burning? How about the lady with all the dirty parrots, the girl with the potato, the men in their penis pants, where are they? There are lions and tigers I know of, pacing in tiny cages somewhere in Kansas. (I tried to save them later, but I couldn't.) And I would've liked to have told Freddie Mercury that his was the only celebrity death that has ever made me profoundly sad, had he been listening. Rip Taylor, I presume, is still mad at me. And what of that little spotted Grand Rapids cat, and all the people's little unspecial spotted cats, foraging for a clean spot in the litter and dreaming of the rabbits bouncing out in the dusk? And let me not forget the young scientist at the lab in Sacramento who answered our questions about bees and combed his hair so nicely for TV and who staggered, stooped over with two canes, and whose dress shirt, tucked in, billowed around his skinny shoulders, and whose single gold band made me think, "Oh, someone loves him. Someone at home loves him. Like someone at home loves me." And tell me, where are my friends, the time-traveling dentist, the bingo cop, the mime in the flooded basement? They can't all still be here, can they? Still?

ADDENDUM

Five years later, I was on another plane, flying across the country for another basic cable show. I was on my way to meet a couple in Maryland with five thousand Cabbage Patch Kids. Their favorite was eighteen-year-old "Kevin," whom they dressed in all kinds of outfits and took with them wherever they went. They spoke to him, and the husband did Kevin's voice when Kevin answered. Their trailer had a $100,000 climate-controlled addition to house all the dolls, but Kevin had his own room. This couple had spent the last eighteen years giving Kevin things their real, human daughter had to work to earn herself (money, clothes, a car). When she finally moved across the country (and into the home of the former drummer of Ratt), her parents couldn't wait to turn her old room into a Cabbage Patch shrine. This was too easy.

And not only that, there were now two new flavors of Luna bars. Even though we'd only been off the ground for ten minutes, I had to have one. I dug around in my carry-on and came across my tube of Protopic—a new nonsteroid topical cream for eczema that's supposed to keep your skin from thinning, and just in time, too. The years of topical steroids had left their mark—little trails on my inner arms where, if you look closely, you can see that the skin is altered, just a bit eroded, as if by streams that later dried up. But if this new medication worked as well for me as it did in clinical trials, I might be able to thicken up and finally get out from under the thumb of Sweet Cousin Cortisone.

I located one of the new Lunas: Caramel Apple, which promised to "rekindle the memories of an irresistible old-fashioned treat." But I was dying to try the other new flavor: Dulce de Leche, which had "all the flavor of the decadent South American dessert in a convenient bar." It was then I remembered I had put it in a special compartment for the St. Louis-to-Baltimore leg. "There you are, you little bastard," I whispered as I ripped off the wrapper and dove in. Mmmm, the decadence! This shoot was going to be a piece of dulce de leche, and it was okay. These people were fucking crazy.

THE EASIER WAY,

FOR EVERYONE

How I hate the twenty-first century, and its very late nights, when the birth control commercial comes on. It's for Ortho Tri-Cyclen Lo, a newish birth control pill that has a low level of estrogen and a low occurrence of the side effects most often associated with oral contraceptives. Its icon is sort of an overturned flower that is also a woman with a budlike, plumed head, and stem torso and limbs, and downward petals that form a skirt. She, the impossible flower-ingenue, ends the commercial by wafting in on a breeze and coming to rest, daintily splayed, atop the company logo: *Tra, la.*

The real girls in the commercial are all about twenty, reedy, and dressed in silky sacks of heather, rose, pewter, mulberry, pistachio, and periwinkle, which, I like to think, are also their names. They pirouette, assume fearless yoga postures, and twinkle as they laugh. They are Creation's bridesmaids. This all happens against a cover of a jangly, singsongy pop song called "There She Goes" by a late–early nineties band called The La's. It goes, *There she goes, there she goes again,* and it feels like tripping through clouds made of daffodils. It sounds like what I remember to be the sweet, petally slip of those nineties. The ones that started out so nicely.

I was around twenty when I started on the pill. I lived alone in a cottage-like apartment in Sherman Oaks that was clean and happy. The owners had just installed new powder blue carpeting in the living room and bedroom, but the entryway still had a strip of original hardwood in which I took great pride and defended with my life. I bought special cleaner for it before I even moved in.

The minute I got the keys, I brought over a vacuum and lovingly drew up the loose little blue scraps that remain when a carpet is that new, that fervent. The living room remained empty nearly the whole time I lived there.

All you could see out the living room window was the bright, bushy midsection of an orange tree. The bedroom window was similarly shrouded, but by pink roses. My bed was clothed in white cotton Battenburg lace, the most ordinary lace, but it was exactly what I wanted. To have a white bed, I thought, was everything.

My bathroom and kitchen had the original tiles that were common to L.A. apartments. The mauve and maroon bathroom was one of 300,000 at least, but I thought it so special: the perfectly clean old porcelain tub.

In I'd waft, late at night, a sprightly little English major in purple and gold suede shoes, and immediately fill that tub with hot, clear water and Crabtree & Evelyn rose bubble bath. I'd sink down in and listen to Billie Holiday or Chet Baker. Sometimes Big Star.

A friend told me that I led a charmed life. I didn't know what that meant. I had to look it up.

Outside a grocery store, I picked a little brown-black kitten from a litter of brown-black kittens and took him to our new home. I bought him special kitten food that came in a pink milk carton. (They don't make it anymore.)

The best thing I could imagine to do was to sit in the empty living room with little Bosco and look at the wide orange leaves and the round orange oranges while peripherally noting the glow of the wood entry, which smelled of Murphy Oil Soap, and anticipate all the black turtlenecked conversations I'd soon be having with people over cappuccinos. I did love cappuccinos, frothy ones.

There we three were: me, carpet, and kitten, unstained, untrampled, unfurled, starting out together. We bristled with options. We could do anything. I put a chest of drawers in my kitchen—for no reason! I just liked it there! I was free to cultivate my own style of handwriting, add an uncalled-for flare to the b's, if I pleased. I could dress myself in fanciful collars, gather wildflowers, make crepes. I was twenty, took the pill, and had my own place with an entryway. I could grow orchids, or just act like I did. I could roll my r's, or adopt a Castilian lisp when it suited me. I could shop at the store for my things.

And I was moved, one night post-bath, to write, quickly and zestfully, a poem. A poem about how I felt. I remember it went mostly like this (the line breaks are inexact):

I push the pill marked "Monday" through the foil and sink
Back into the flowered sheets, pink and moss
[something here?] my [wet or damp] hair mingles with
    the [probably "leaves"]
And my faucet leaks
Each moment I'm here and each moment I'm gone
[I probably expanded on that a bit here]
[something about] my kitten breaks the cactus
and bats the stems with his paws
And my faucet leaks
I could collect the water,
And use it for the plant
I could put the water to use
But instead I gather the [broken stems?] and put them
Back in the pot.
Put the pot on the sill
And take Tuesday's pill

There's a lot going on there. We've got an awareness of the passage of time, of waste, of fertility, of wasted fertility, of idleness, of guilt, of more waste, of downright sloth, the prick of the cactus (abortion) needle (the catalyst for the pill), aridity (the Poet as Broken Cactus), irony (the two-dimensional flora encased in linen mockingly juxtaposed to my three-dimensional fertility), helplessness, bliss, mortality, pharmaceuticals. Though, I don't think describing the cactus as having stems was meant to be ironic. I was just a little dumb.

But, I seemed to know I was in my blooming phase, and I seem to have thought it was a real grind.

Some backstory: my bathroom faucet leaked (in my poetry, things are sometimes exactly what they appear to be), and I was at a loss about how to handle it. I didn't know this was the sort of thing that could be fixed by someone without plumber's credentials. I had no one, or thought I had no one (a guy, with tools), to consult. Dad, brother, boyfriends, all absent in some way. My only option was to tell the off-site building manager, a nasally guy named Russell Sepulveda. But I couldn't do that because he might find out about Bosco and I wasn't supposed to have pets. So I took my oral contraceptives, closed the bathroom door, and wrote poems.

My eldest sister really thought that I should have some kind of furniture in the living room. A great hander-down of wicker was Lee Grenrock, and this white, cushionless living room set (a loveseat, a chair, a coffee table) was just the first wicker she had in store for me. A couple years later, she'd give me a dead man's trunk that I'd use for a coffee table for too long.

I hated this hard, splintery stuff and neither Bosco nor I understood why we needed it. There were things we just didn't need. The carpet was soft and new! And just because *society* said that you had to have a couch . . . but okay, I thought, so some sun-bleached furniture shipwrecked itself in my little cove. I'll try to sit on it.

I tried to sit on it.

And then the men came with the unasked-for air conditioner and cut the hole in the wall that broke my heart.

A month or so later, I was mugged by some child gangsters with a sawed-off shotgun. It was late at night when I was leaving the record store where I worked on Melrose Avenue. These guys had my keys, my address, everything, so a few days later, I moved in with an ex-junkie rock singer whom I had just started seeing. I liked his band, they had been popular in L.A. for a few years, but I barely knew anything about him.

The first time we spoke, as he walked me from the record store to get a gelato one evening, he told me he had just gotten out of rehab. I didn't even know what the word meant. I had to look it up.

I was recovering from an abortion from a one-night stand (I'd tired of the demands of the pill) when he happened to telephone. He came over to my apartment and immediately turned on that air conditioner. He flung open the windows, cleaned the cat box, and lit some of his "new favorite incense." It did smell nice, island-y. He kept it going through the beginning of our relationship, at his place and mine. It did smell nice. I fell for that smell pretty hard.

The entryway of the house he shared with the singer of the Circle Jerks was covered in simulated wood-grain linoleum. My bath mat didn't match his bathroom. My lace bedding stayed in a box. His dogs fought with Bosco so he made Bosco sleep in a separate room and I LET HIM. I LET A GUY WITH A RECORD DEAL COME BETWEEN ME AND MY CAT. THE CAT THAT I

RAISED ON KITTEN FOOD THAT CAME IN THE PINK MILK CARTON. THE CAT THAT SAT IN THE KITCHEN WINDOW AT NIGHT WAITING FOR ME TO COME HOME.

The last thing I saw my cat do was jump on the counter, rip a tortilla out of this new boyfriend's hand, and dash out the front door. I looked and looked and looked for him.

Soon, the guy went back to drugs so I went with him, and then went back for more. There I went, there I went again, frittering away too much of the nineties—the ones that had started for me so nicely, when Julia Roberts and I shared a head of hair and I sometimes put on a cozy sweater in the mornings and held my cup of coffee with both hands, not knowing what that La's song was even about.

We were just a scum couple now. [Sample argument: "I fucking pay for shit all the time! Who bought you those shoes?" "You want these fucking shoes? Here, take your fucking shoes!" And he'd take one of my fucking shoes and throw it out the window of the car (speeding downtown for more drugs), and there my little black clog would stay, in the middle of the street.]

I guess I spent the nineties doing some appropriate things (crack was smoked, there were rock stars), but everything was going so fast, and knowing how creep leads on to creep, I doubted if I should ever come back.

Flashing forward quite a few years finds me hovering around Glucose Cove, the name I have for the waiting area just off the pharmacy section at one of the big new supermarkets here in Hollywood. I call it that because it always looks like its only contents: sugar-free mint melt-a-ways, sugar-free truffles, disrespected diabetes brochures, and a small veneered sitting area, which are regularly tousled by slow washes of seawater and stay that way until the next swell comes and rearranges them again. That day, an old man was sitting in the Cove filling out flu shot paperwork at the drifted-together end table and one of the two chairs. All around him were hearing aid batteries and things with fake sugar. Meters, pumps, sad things. It's miserable to behold, but as a pharmacy service, it's more than sufficient. Everything is always ready when they say it will be and the pharmacists (all ladies) are kind and diligent. Especially Beth. Beth's great.

I was there to gather my birth control pills, plus a couple extra prescriptions I've netted over the last few years. There was a line at the register, a rarity, so in my head I was going over my lines for tomorrow's TV shoot. I was to be playing a teacher on the WB's long-running hit show called *7th Heaven*. It'd been on since '96, but I'd never seen it, and all I knew was that there were a lot of people on it and they comprised some sort of Christian family. I thought maybe it had something to do with a retarded kid named Corky and his tolerant sister, but I may have been confusing it with some other show.

When I had woken up a few mornings earlier, the idea of playing a teacher on *7th Heaven* had never even entered my mind, but by the end of the day, I was to play a teacher on *7th Heaven*. The job was offered to me and I took it. How my name ever came up to play a teacher on an Aaron Spelling–produced Christian family show on the WB network was too heavy a question for me. I can't think about things like that too hard.

I don't think about things like that too hard.

"Reverend Camden, this is Gina Allison, from Ruthie's school. I'm the sponsor of the school newspaper staff."

That was my first line from my first scene and I was so afraid I was going to mess it up. I was telephoning Reverend Camden and identifying myself as the sponsor of the school newspaper staff at Ruthie's school.

"Reverend Camden, this is Gina Allison, from Ruthie's school. I'm the sponsor of the school newspaper staff."

I gathered that Ruthie was a school-aged girl, and the charge of this Camden fellow, a reverend.

But what was the "sponsor of the school newspaper staff"? Did it mean, like, the head of it? The "sponsor" sounded like she paid for the newspaper, she bankrolled it. On a teacher's salary? It hardly seemed possible. What was I not getting about Gina Allison?

"Reverend Camden, this is Gina Allison, from Ruthie's school. I'm the sponsor of the school newspaper staff."

I thought if I could just get that first line out, I'd be okay, but every time I drilled it farther into my head, my head wanted to say "newspaper squad" instead of "staff." I hoped I could pull it together at the moment of truth, at action time.

A woman pushed an overburdened cart up the main aisle. She had it crammed so full of stuff that it made the ragged silhouette of a jalopy puttering across the Dust Bowl. Her matte black pigtails scrambled over her softsweatered shoulders. I caught myself staring—looking on in judgment at all the Hamburger Helper and two-liter bottles of Squirt jutting out the sides and bottom of the cart. Everything about her bespoke the trauma of bulk buying. She was weary at the helm, only able to initiate the smallest movements necessary to set the wheels in motion, like the tortured heft of pudding as it boils. People drifted out from her. She was headed for Glucose Cove.

She had seen me staring at her and was looking back quizzically. The Cove wasn't empty, there was that old flu shot man in there, and she wasn't having it. I knew, because she shouted about it from twenty feet away.

"I usually use this area for cart reorganization," she said, eyes rolling, "but now!"

Okay, I thought, time to disengage. That loud, public proclamation, and a closer look at the dusty pigtails and the stained elastic-waist pants, had prompted my survival gene to perk up and drain any rising concern out of my expression. I turned my gaze seamlessly away to rest on the diabetes brochures.

I assume everyone has some kind of automatic public lunatic release system. It's animalistic. If one African wild dog were to suddenly come back from a hunt with a faraway look in his eyes and start spouting off some nonsense about Kahlil Gibran, black helicopters, and using Paul McCartney as his personal toilet, the other African wild dogs would all sense that something was amiss and turn away casually, pretending to look at some diabetes brochures.

However, I could still feel her presence. I could feel her mind and body debating: "What to do, what to do. Gotta reorganize the cart, can't reorganize the cart, but gotta reorganize the cart," whatever that meant.

She navigated her way into the Cove after all, and took the empty chair. Then, pushing aside a few cardboard advertisements for blood pressure medicines and a display of little free magazines with the headline "Eva Longoria—for the Love of Children" from the end table, she began cart reorganization efforts. One by one, with the alacrity of the big crane that picks the toys out of the glass box, she lifted and considered each item from the cart.

While talking.

"You can fit eight times as much in if you organize it right," she told the flu shot man.

Ah, he said.

"Oh, yeah. I have coupons for it all."

Aahh.

"I do all my shopping once a month."

Hmmmm.

It was during her first long speech ("I go around and get the things, but I can't reorganize until I have half of everything, and then I come in here to organize it all because you can fit six times as much in if you organize it right," etc.) that I noticed she was sitting in front of a rack of what are called "self-care" products. This series was called "Enablers" and their slogan was: *The easier way, for everyone.* There were door openers, jar openers, zipper pulls, button helpers, light switch finders, key enlargers. My life was still charmed to the extent of never having seen such things. They were more or less plastic or rubber extenders to be affixed to an object to make it bigger, friendlier, less complicated. I pictured my parents, Vic and Char, getting an Enabler, the zipper-puller perhaps, and becoming confused about how to get the damn thing on the zipper. And I saw myself, on my next visit, witnessing a reenactment of the ordeal and endorsing the irony that the zipper-puller actually makes it *harder* to pull the zipper up. Char would be so annoyed and want to return the damn thing, but Vic would be enjoying the telling of the story too much. He'd write a funny letter to the Enabler people that he would read to everyone, but never send.

"I do my shopping once a month," our pigtailed friend shouted. "Oh yeah, I'll be here all day."

The end table had become the foundation for a kind of Hamburger Helper citadel, with its grand Tuna Helper tower flanked by a Cheesy Pasta grotto and a botanical garden of a box of something called Suddenly Salad. On the outskirts of town it looked like she had begun work on an industrial zone of Campbell's soup cans: all the same kind, the very rare Cream of Shrimp.

Campbell's soup. My God, did *everything* relate back to Gina Allison?

My role, Gina's role, as sponsor of the school newspaper *staff*, was to facilitate and foster the collection of Campbell's soup can labels from all the students in order to procure a new computer for use by the school newspaper *staff*. Gina Allison had some sort of arrangement with the Campbell's soup people that made this so, I assumed, and the producers of *7th Heaven* had some arrangement of their own.

Propelling the soup label subplot seemed to be the

function of Gina Allison, as far as I could tell. This, and to add her concern to the growing pile of concern surrounding the recent knocking-up of young Ruthie, about which Reverend Camden was about to set her straight. Reading the provided script didn't answer anything for me, but that was partially my fault—every time I tried to read it, my eyes glazed over and crossed and eventually led the rest of me to sleep. I didn't understand who all these characters were and why they were doing and saying what they were. And where was the retarded kid? I didn't see him anywhere.

When I finally got up to the front, Beth wasn't there. Instead, it was that other lady whose eyes were big and glassy, with purple-veined lids sheer as fly's wings. She was less agreeable than Beth or the other pharmacist, who looks like Marisa Tomei. Once, the three of us had shared a nice laugh over how much harder Beth worked than she did and how willing Beth was to go the "extra mile." Marisa Tomei was just about to put in a call to my physician, and I said, Oh, trying to show up Beth, eh? and she laughed, saying, Yes! I guess so! and Beth had overheard this and laughed as well.

This other pharmacist told me that for whatever reason, my doctor had not done something, and something else to do with insurance, or something, and therefore, something was not ready. It would be a few minutes, she said, so I wandered around the store.

This was a vast supermarket in a flat, seething part of the city. It was big, and sold big things. Everything on the shelves appeared to me hazardous and unloving. Barbed plastic packaging. Putrid colors. Abusive insignias. Combat-ive cartoon characters. I Hate You Cola, Bitch Wafers, Sad Man Prepared Entrées. Even Suddenly Salad was emit-ting little rays of scorn.

I'd grown used to my safe, boutique-y markets with their barreled dry goods and community kindliness. Kenny and I sometimes giddily mock the contents of our very own cupboards: "Do we have any more Uncle Teddy's All Nat-ural Organic Fig Burrows? What about those Molasses Goddess Earth Magic Ginger Bars? Oh, no! We're nearly out of Paul's Amazing Salt." These items, individually held and hand-tagged by a thoughtful person, had ingredients lists that read like poems by progressive schoolchildren: "Made from organic stone-ground corn, expeller-pressed olive oil, life, light, and love for all the world! To your health! Peace to all beings."

No, no, these menacing supermarket superitems wouldn't do at all. Too many intrusions into the psyche, not enough thought given to sustaining the natural order. Not good, certainly not good for the bears, the fish, the meerkats, the seahorses, the egrets, the otters, the others.

And I do love the bears, the fish, the meerkats, the egrets, all those otters, every seahorse and all their brothers and sis-ters in the kingdom. I've always thought of them and how they feel. My one-woman crusade against Colonel Sanders was inspired by the loveliness I noticed in some chickens I met in a backyard in San Diego. (They just let you hold them, you know.) A drive along any city street or country road so often had me worried, upon seeing unkempt grounds or smoke- and sebum-smudged city windows,

What horror lay beyond this? How many unknown pets could be silently stifling inside? Thirsty dogs? Tick-filled cats? Neglected fish in boggy tanks? Finches too close to a heater or not close enough? Finches, eight to a cage, on the balcony? It got to be where I thought of nothing else. I wanted nothing to hurt. I'd try to softly scoop the summer ants from the kitchen counter onto a paper towel for relocation outside. I'd sit and think, and think and think, about their colonies and how best to honor them. But somewhere, behind a wall, tethered to some post, will always be some dying dog and it will be unknown to me. There would never be an end to suffering.

Anyway, they found a drug for me.

It was just a few weeks before that I had begun my dalliance with the selective serotonin reuptake inhibiting family of drugs, the SSRI's, and so far, it was working out fine. I was experiencing an overall Silence of the Finches, but there remained a healthy empathy for all the sentient beings, confirmed still by the periodic and much easier writing of tax-deductible donation checks. (Besides, one must ask, would the cessation of all the world's suffering itself bring about the ultimate suffering? For if there is no suffering, and all living things just quietly disintegrate at some point in their lives, would it then *be* life? What makes something have life? And is the absence of this thing itself the ultimate suffering? I'll bet Reverend Camden knew.)

This is how I've come to understand SSRI's: In the brain there's serotonin, which makes you happy, but if you spend part of your life, perhaps your There She Goes years, altering your brain's chemistry, you may end up altering your brain's chemistry. And if you are also predisposed to need to take an even number of steps while boarding a plane because you fear that not to do so could bring about the death of us all, it's even worse. So, they give you a pill that regulates your serotonin, and sometimes it helps.

I recently saw a TV show about some brain researchers who had just gotten a groovy new brain slicer for their lab that allowed them to make these tissue-thin slices of brain, thinner than ever before and way, way thinner than the slicer in the deli section can make on its thinnest setting.

In the brain slices, the scientists were able to isolate what looked to me like purple seahorse tails and snouts but was really the hormone serotonin. They showed one slice in which every centimeter was flooded with purple seahorse bits. Oh good, you think, that must've been a very happy person. No, it turned out to be the schizophrenic guy's brain. The seahorses need to be regulated. This is where the selective serotonin reuptake inhibitors come in. They are like pharmaceutical doormen—big bald pills in black suits and black T-shirts who stand with a clipboard and an earpiece and tell your serotonin, "No ins and outs," and "I can't let anyone else in until some people leave."

I, like so many of my comrades from the nineties, just needed this extra push from glum to glam, but what was the pill for the pigtailed shopper who'd be here all day? I was afraid of blowing lines on a TV show, but what was this lady's thing? She was just doing her shopping in a folksy way. Too folksy? What made her this way? Was Hamburger Helper not giving her the helping hand she needed? Perhaps this fell outside the reach of what that nimble little gloved hand with a face was able to do.

The people on the SSRI Web sites express their individuality while living and working and going to engagement parties In The City. They have mostly good memories of Lollapalooza and will sometimes wear hats. They think a guy in the building is kinda cute. Of course they know what a tomatillo is. They're not crazy, they would just like their lives back. And, if all goes well, they will blossom gracefully into the people in the gardening hats and clogs on the cholesterol-lowering-pill Web sites. They will acquire second homes and think each other every bit as beautiful on their silver anniversaries as they were when they first laid eyes on each other. They will mark the passage of time with diamonds.

But which pill does one take if one is just sort of dirty and weird? Just sort of bizarre and unkempt? Who's on your Web site? Who's your mascot? Shelley Winters?

I was standing in the makeup aisle and thinking of buying Maybelline Illegal Lengths mascara in brownish black when the music paused briefly (had it been playing "Imagine"?) and a prerecorded voice broke in: "Do you misplace your keys? It could be common forgetfulness, but it could be something far more serious."

The voice reminded us shoppers to consult our doctors if we suspected that it might be something far more serious than common forgetfulness. And then the music started again.

I forgot things all the time. I had forgotten Alanis Morissette's name just a few days earlier. I saw her face in my head, clear as day, represented in an accurate succession of her more notable hairstyles, but her name simply would not come. She was looking at me, bug-eyed, with a naive sort of longing, and saying, "Stacey, it's me, ———— ——! You know me! It's A—n—la—Mah—tt. Come on, Stace! You *know* this, of course you do!"

At the frozen section, a clear package of what looked like a pile of skulls at the Tuol Sleng Genocide Museum in Phnom Penh caught my eye. Thankfully, they were just dumplings, pale little cocoons of food, but they got me thinking about memory. Suppose memories were dumplings, like cocoons of thoughts. Little steamy sachets of minced matter and feelings: animal, vegetable, mineral, all festering and indistinguishable until you revive them in a pot of hot wa—oh, this was a terrible theory. One of the worst I'd ever had. Far-reaching and pointless. I dismissed this stupid theory and kept wandering.

These pills seemed to be making my memory worse. Certain seahorses were getting lost in my hippocampus. And there were so many things I couldn't risk forgetting, besides Gina Allison's issues. Like the Ecstasy parties in Ibiza back in '89. Gotta keep those.

I'd heard from a friend that if you try to take Ecstasy on SSRI's, nothing happens. The surge of serotonin is no match for the big bald inhibitors and their clipboards. I'd just have to hold on tightly to those unearthly joyous feelings, most recently played out a few years ago in the Mojave Desert. I remember the sky being so pitch black and so flooded with hot stars as to appear comical. Surely, I thought, this is not the sky I've been looking at all my life.

This is some sort of precious school-play sky set from a Wes Anderson movie. And not only that, the twinkling stars are plinking out a tune on a child-sized piano. Heavens, we have all become children again! It's really happening just the way I would dream it. Earth is lovely, and so is breathing this hot air that is holding me up with just its heat. That's all! And who's that guy in the Scandinavian cap, that beautiful Scandinavian cap? He's a friend! Awww. I have so many friends. There's Peggy, loving her little socks, look at her over there. And someone else is touching the faucet stream. I love the faucet stream, too. Do I want to put my fingers in it, too? Yes, I do! We laugh, and I can see my laughs escape my mouth, all of our mouths, up there in the bungalow loft while we unknowingly chafe our elbows on the old gold carpet. Hey! Did that other guy find the switch for the hot tub? What is the status of that, does anyone know? Where are you going, I'm coming with you. I'm taking your hand and coming with you. Here we go, we are friends! Are we going in the hot tub? I love hot tubs.

Those were nice times. Just like the first nights with a new kitten, watching him explore his new home and figure out how to get on the bed when it's time to go to sleep. (He hinges his little claws to the bedspread and climbs up and then he settles in to the softest spot right in the middle and falls fast asleep, purring so loud it keeps you awake.) Wow, that's a good one. Please, don't inhibit that. And please let me keep the milk carton, the pink milk carton. They don't make it anymore.

"Reverend Camden, this is Gina Allison, from Ruthie's school. Did you misplace your keys?"

Those things remind me of my very first private bathroom, which I have mentioned, with its mauve and maroon tile and its very white tub. After a short night of sweet and pretty pursuits (work, school, friends, flirtation, White Russians, hair twirling, vintage dress wearing), that bath was such a nice way to warm up. I miss the feeling of being twenty and buying my own bath mat, finally getting to pick color, shape, and density. How it really defined the room, and how my toes looked on it. (A bit like a baby koala's.)

I miss big roses and big oranges outside my window. That air conditioner ruined the whole scene.

"Reverend Camden, Gina Allison. We met through Ruthie. Reverend Camden, it could be something far more serious."

But the taste of cold corn tortillas and old peanut butter for days on end alone in someone else's apartment because I had no other place to go and not even a dollar? That I could gladly forget. As well as the muzzled stray poodle I saw out the car window wandering the streets of Paris that haunts me to this day. Even if he found food, I thought, he couldn't eat it. Mom, Mom, look at that poodle! Shouldn't we stop and help that poodle? But what could I do? I was just a child tourist in a fast-moving cab.

And while I'm at it, I could also do without the way my dining room set looked out on the sidewalk (where the marshals had put it that terrible morning in 1993), the lies I told my parents, the sweet German shepherd I ignored (the sound of her cries from where she stood tied at the side of the house), the dolls I got mad at and threw in the closet (the way they seemed to look at me afterward, just before I shut the door), the dust and semen smell of single guys' apartments, the considerable heft of chain bookstore brownies, diarrhea on a stranger's lawn, *front* lawn (broad daylight, no less), the junkie girl in that apartment with the black walls on a Saturday afternoon who sat spackling and respackling Joe Blasco concealer into the cavern left by a cigarette burn on her face (she'd been doing it for hours), rubber cement self-applied to the backs of my adolescent water-jug ears, a history of earthquakes, going back to the cradle.

"Reverend Camden, I'm so sorry, I realize now that wasn't my line. My line is 'Reverend Camden, this is Gina Allison, from Ruthie's school. I'm the sponsor of the school newspaper squad STAFF.' Please, Reverend, I'm sure it's just common forgetfulness, not something far more serious. Please believe me! It's Gina, by the way."

EVA LONGORIA—FOR THE LOVE OF CHILDREN! WILL THIS EVER STOP?

Psst-ing at me from the magazine rack, out from behind a quarterly rag called *Short Hairstyles,* was an issue of *Cooking Light.* I was familiar with this magazine. I had complimented a holiday dessert called something like "crumbling berry slump," as one does when one is a guest in one's in-laws' home in Arizona, and faster than you could carve the words "Bela Lugosi's Dead" into your forearm, I had myself a year's subscription to the publication from whence the recipe came. Every month, I learned so many things I wish I didn't still know. There are so many ways to spice up skinless chicken breasts. There are so many occasions to replace fat with applesauce. I cried every time it arrived in my mailbox. Two thousand two. It was my year of cooking light.

I was leafing through some weekly, noting the crumbled marriage of Jennifer Aniston, admiring Mariska Hargitay's Emmy dress, when I noticed that next to me, thumbing through *Child,* was a mustached man in a T-shirt that said "I Love Jesus and Jesus Loves You." I love Jesus and Jesus loves you—he served as the middle link of a chain. See, it's a standard relevance logic theorem: If I love Jesus, then Jesus loves you. Therefore, if I do not love Jesus, then Jesus does not love you. If A, then B, therefore if not A, then not B. $(A \rightarrow B :: >A \rightarrow >B)$. I learned it in junior college.

Back at the Cove, the line was gone, and the pigtailed woman sat restacking alone. I picked up my pharmaceuticals without incident and left.

There was my boring old birth control pill (lowest of the low hormones, which I was beginning to suspect I didn't even need anymore, now that my blooming phase had peaked), the reinvigorated SSRI's, and a new, slightly suspicious sleeping pill that I was eager to try that night.

Insomniacs such as I find it impossible to conjure anything like sleep on the night before a big day. Tomorrow was a big day that started early. Up to this time, I had no idea that a person could just tell a doctor, "I have trouble sleeping sometimes," and get a prescription for a sleep aid. I thought they gave you some sort of test or called your mom at least.

Having this pill made me feel a bit dastardly, driving home with it in my purse felt faintly illegal. Ambien. I'd heard of it, I'd seen the commercials for it. It wasn't the one with the butterfly that flew around the town and fluttered everyone to sleep, but it was similar to that one. It did similar things to a similar town.

I had to get up really early to get to *7th Heaven,* so Kenny and I watched *Law & Order: SVU* in bed. (It was about death and sex, body parts in trash bags, something.) Then I took my Ambien and I remember nothing that happened after that.

I'm told that while appearing wide awake, I started talking about a trapeze artist that only I saw on our bedroom television. What was actually on TV was a documentary about the Yugoslav wars that I found riotously funny. I loved all the trapeze work in it.

But nothing could've prepared me for the dreams I would have on this drug. There were three, and they were all about prime-time television.

Ambien Dream 1

Starring Jennifer Aniston, Stavros Anistas,
and Stacey Grenrock Woods

Actress Jennifer Aniston was employed as an object of ritual sex torture by her cunning, densely mustached father, Stavros Anistas. It had been going on since her girlhood, and she had chosen this time to tell me, some sort of static observer/consciousness-being, all the details. At first I wasn't convinced, until I saw what Stavros did to poor Jennifer on a regular, practically nightly basis—I saw our Jen, little Rachel Green, strung up by one foot above a rather satanic bed and wrapped tightly, in permanent arabesque, by a massive length of clean, thick rope. Her face, her eyes, completely covered. She was cocooned, in an S&M cocoon, by her nasty Greek, folksinging father.

Indeed, Stavros Anistas was one half of an obscure but influential folk/glam/art happening collective in the seventies. He was the dark half, and there was a blond half, who came over later, for the orgy, and turned dark and curly when he was made, for the amusement of Anistas, to shoot heroin directly into his own brain tissue (which I also witnessed and which took place in the half-bath of my childhood home, the one we always called "the little bathroom").

Back to Jen, hanging there. She was her father's sexual prisoner, still in her rope cocoon. She was made to do this so often, it was beyond belief. It was horrible to behold. He never let her use birth control and she was forever going to the clinic for her abortions. I thought, "When this gets out, and it will, Brad and Angelina are going to feel really, really bad about what they've done."

Jen wrote scrapbooks of poems about how it felt to be enclosed. The poems were epic, and the fonts changed subtly throughout the poems, but her fucking father, her fucking Greek, mustached cunt of a father, stole her work and passed it off as his folk songs. She wanted me to read them, but I couldn't. They were too sad and to ingest them would have caused my body harm.

But if you think Stavros Anistas is bad, you should meet Jen's mother (no name). It was her sicko edict that had instilled itself in Jen at such a young age: the philosophy that "It's okay to have sex with your father occasionally for extra money." Can you believe that?

Jen hated her dad, but she really hated her mom. Her wiry, conniving little mom.

Then Jen and I were trying on tops in a hip little store. We shared a dressing room, and I was shocked by her smallness and the ruddiness of her shoulders and chest. "People probably don't know the ruddiness of her," I thought. "They must golden her up for magazines and public appearances." And her rib cage, like a child's! Her too large head was like a doll's in every way except that it had furrow lines and frown lines, and the rouge stippling sprayed up the sides of her neck. She tried on feminine top after feminine top, finally deciding on a few breezy, salmon- and pistachio-colored silky things. She said she might as well be comfortable and feel pretty, she had a long night ahead of her.

Ambien Dream 2

*Starring: Mariska Hargitay and Chris Meloni
from* Law & Order: SVU, *Stacey Grenrock Woods,
and Seymour Cassell as Chris Meloni*

Word had just come through that poor old Seymour Cassell, the nice old guy who played Chris Meloni in Chris Meloni's life so that Chris Meloni was free to play Detective Elliot Stabler on TV's *Law & Order: SVU,* had died. We all felt sad, because we all really liked him, and also, Chris Meloni had to be Chris Meloni now.

And then Chris Meloni died.

But, inexplicably, I was walking around a time-share I time-shared with his costar, Mariska Hargitay (I think it was in a lake community, possibly Havasu in Arizona), and seeing Chris everywhere I looked. There he was, slicing tomatoes on the birchwood countertop, getting everyone jazzed up about his "famous salsa," fiddling with the VCR, organizing newspaper inserts.

"Mariska?" I said.

"Psst, Mariska? Why is everyone saying Chris is dead? He's not dead—look, he's got a tomatillo in his very real, Italian and French-Canadian actor hand!"

"Oh," she said, "see, Chris is dead, but he's one of those doesn't-know-it dead people."

"So, he's stuck here in this time-share?"

"Yes, until he figures out and accepts that even though he is an actor, or was an actor, he can't get anyone else to act the part of death for him. And he can't act dead, he has to *be* dead."

It was making sense, finally. She also told me that every time I thought of Chris, I was conjuring him, thereby confusing him and making it even harder for him to move on. I had to stop thinking of him.

Well, it was kind of hard with him standing there recording *Ryan's Hope* and making snacks like that!

She said we should go shopping.

Mariska and I were really becoming friends, but I was still wary of the kinds of stores she wanted to browse around in. I'd feel my chest tense every time we passed one of those easy-breezy-beautiful-ladies-in-flowing-hand-dyed-silk-and-lace stores. I was afraid Mariska wanted to stop in and make me try on some kind of *Accidental Tourist* getup.

I said I wanted to find a store where they sold Spring Court tennis shoes—the kind John Lennon used to wear. French tennis shoes.

She laughed a little, and said I was a dreamer.

Back in the control room, the technician showed me a Claymation image of Chris Meloni's head, where the striving-for-life parts were represented by more detail than the accepting-death parts. He showed on a time line how, the less I thought about him, the more blurred and impressionistic the head became. We could see it happening. I was sent to the end of the room to not think about Chris for a few minutes and I didn't.

"See? Look now," said the technician. Chris's head was just some green clay, with those hazy blue veiled-over fetus ponds where the eyes once were. He was blurring, he was ghosting. He was going off to the ghost place. He was blue, he was green, he felt better. He was truly, truly being dead.

Ambien Dream 3

Chris Meloni has invented a game!

In the game, each player must go out and collect trash. Then, each player brings his collected trash to the Trash Meeting Point, where it is judged by all players and a decision about its worth is made mutually.

I collect some maroon Polarfleece vest parts, a pile of twigs, and a paper soda cup that says "Giant Slurp" on it.

My father, Vic, finds glossy black trash bags, two of them.

Chris Meloni finds an empty VCR box that he figures he can sell.

My mother finds no trash, but is informed while she is out looking that my father is distantly related to Jodie Foster. She shows off a plastic photo wallet insert with old family photos and a missing picture.

"See that?" she says.

"Yes, it's nothing, an empty space."

She shook her head. "That's the difference between us," she said. "You see an empty space, I see where Jodie Foster should be."

There was a lot going on there, but I had no time to dissect it. It was five-fifteen and time for me to go to the set of *7th Heaven*.

Still shaking off the television dreams, I was met with the aftermath of what I had done in the kitchen during the night. In between dream states, I must've gotten hungry. Scattered all over the counter and floor was a killing field of tortilla chips—the ones made from organic stone-ground corn, expeller-pressed olive oil, life, light, and love for all the world. There was also an open can of Tuscan beans that had been partially dribbled into a pot that I had taken down from the pot rack, apparently, and set on the stove. I didn't recall doing any of this, but there I had been, the evidence showed, all alone in the kitchen, cooking dark.

But at least I had fallen asleep quickly enough to be spared the nightly sorrow of that Ortho Tri-Cyclen Lo commercial.

I left the house at 5:45, allowing an hour (ample, ample time) to get to the deep San Fernando Valley to the weird, wood-paneled, adobe-style *7th Heaven* compound. At 6:25 I got a call. It was the assistant director, wondering where I was.

"But my call is six forty-five!"

"No, actually, your call was at six-fifteen."

Six-fifteen?!

"No, the guy told me yesterday when he called that it was six forty-five!"

"Nope. Six-fifteen."

"Well, I was told six forty-five."

"Well, if you could get here as soon as possible, that would be great, okay?"

I was told 6:45.

Every cell in my body wanted to tell every single person on the set that it was not my fault. But I refrained. (Zoloft, thank you.)

I arrived on the set to an even greater horror: "Gina" Allison had become "Regina" Allison. No one even told me. I found out when I got to my trailer, after I stepped into my wardrobe: fitted short-sleeve "cute" jacket, short skirt, knee-high brown leather lace-up boots (it was an Aaron Spelling Christian family show, after all). Had I not glanced at the blue script (meaning "latest") pages that had been left on my table, I wouldn't have caught the name change.

"Reverend Camden, this is REGina Allison . . ."

It was easy to drift off in the hair and makeup trailer. It's nice being touched and complimented by people who want nothing from you. Even having mousse (something I hadn't seen or felt since the nineties, early nineties) worked into my hair by a fellow who looked like Tommy Lee Jones can be a grand thing. So often in these scenarios I'd hope for some kind of work stoppage (power outage, strike, world war) that would have us all go home.

REGina, REGina.

I was half expecting it. It could've been chalked up to any number of pat reasons—nervousness about pissing off the Italians, a clerical error—but the real reason for the name change was pretty clear: Gina Allison was a skank's name. Gina Allisons don't get hired at Ruthie's school. It's the kind of name a girl takes when she starts dancing at Captain Cream's: "Gina" is her first name, and "Allison" because she always liked the name and would've named her daughter that but he turned out to be a boy, oh well! Gina Allison drives a Mazda Miata and reeks of tangy sauce. Most people have bad associations with someone named Gina. Gina brings her dog to the pound when she moves. ("What am I supposed to do? My new place doesn't allow pets.") She is the moral, physical, mental, spiritual result of one thousand Diet Cokes, of eighty weekends getting smashed at Lake Havasu. She's someone you see in line at the payday advance, with her tautly pulled hair, those crisp, ginger-colored worms spiraling down her shoulders, stubborn blackheads, reverse French manicure, and a speck on her ear (what is it? it's near her big earrings). Her sweater has a brothy smell, a hot, cloudy water smell that lives in old apartments. She'll get a manicure before she'll buy baby food. She's everyone you ever turn away from, everyone who causes that silent connection among strangers in a public place. Her sweatpants are dirty, her voice is too loud, her cart is overstuffed, she has a smashed mint cream under her shoe, she's keeping that nice old guy from finishing his flu shot paperwork. (He needs his flu shot! The flu can kill an old guy!) She's too familiar. Why can't the Hamburger Helper hand just extend one of its three fingers up to her mouth and say, "Shhhhhh. No one wants to hear that"?

Hair and makeup done, I was taken on set and situated near Regina Allison's living room. The director, a funny old guy with a list of Aaron Spelling prime-time credits as long as your knee-high boots, introduced himself. He took to me right away when it was revealed through some small talk that I knew who Rene Auberjonois was.

Regina Allison revealed herself as a fan of IKEA. She had a cozy couch, soft lighting, and a birch-veneer coffee table. She had candles. I was inclined to think she had to have back issues of *Cooking Light* catalogued and bound in vinyl, and had made a database of all her favorite recipes where everything is cross-referenced. Regina Allison does those paper bags with a candle in them up the walk (she's got two drawers of tea lights that she opens and thinks, "How cool is *that*?") and after school, she's been planning a Dads and Grads party (she's researching the sort of granita drink she'll serve). I don't know why I hated her so much. Maybe Regina Allison is the person I didn't grow into. The person who would've welcomed the air conditioner. This would truly be a test of my acting prowess. I wanted to quickly think of something about her—some subtext known only to me to add a little authentically human grit—a little gravel in the shoe, if you will, of the character. Should I play her as a racist?

We were about ready to shoot. Regina and I sat on our couch, and picked up our phone. A guy off camera would be feeding me the lines of the good reverend. I was Regina Allison, and I was in my world.

. . . And action!

All was perfectly still and silent as a cocoon.

Wasn't there something I had to tell Reverend Camden? What was it? Why did I call him again?

Back in the trailer, I took off my boots and rubbed my feet. I wondered (but just for a second) how much better Eva Longoria's trailer was than this.

Look at my toes! I was seeing the beginnings of what I thought looked like old-man toenails. Flaky and opaque. I noticed that the Chantilly lace haze of flake on my instep was back. In the corners of my big toenails was dark matter I couldn't bear to address. It's that I couldn't face what it could be, but also that I didn't really care. Also there was the horrible sharp poke and scrape in the corner of the nail bed.

I put those boots back on and waited for my next scene, which would have me acting with Ruthie and some other teens, on the school hallway set, while holding a box of Campbell's soup labels. A different kind of challenge, but at least I'd be able to play off the energy of the other actor, a thirteen-year-old girl named Mackenzie something.

I heard once that you can tell if someone's young or old by pinching the skin on her hand and counting how long it takes to snap back. Time, memory, age, they are all just that—a series of those small times. They happen in the moments, the small, slow moments that it takes the skin on the back of your hand to redrape itself around the bones. It's all just a series of increasingly labored bubbles in pudding. There it goes. There it goes again.

And then we are all the old people in Glucose Cove, whose gums, when they smile, are a cloisonné of salty purple and gray meat with a thin marbling of pus. Whose bald-scalp sores are like a quarry of rubies and some amber chips.

This is how people get old and disappear. They don't all get the best gardening clogs. Some of them just drift off somewhere. It starts there, in the corner of the toe, or in one scraggly eyebrow hair overlooked, or some pesky skin tags that you mean to have seen about but never get around to, that you stop noticing in the mirror. Those things from which it's easier to turn away. And in the world of late there has been a great turning away. A great turning away and looking toward pictures of Eva Longoria.

They caught the gang kids who mugged me a few months later. One of them was driving around with my license on the floor of his car.

My face, before this bit of cheek hollow, had such a glee in that license photo. That layer of subcutaneous face fat, in which the sweetly unaware expression that asks, "Golly, what's up next?" resides, got left on the floor of some gangster's car forever. Subsequent license photos have shown a face that has had a few melt-aways and redrapings around the bones into a new expression that says, "Oh, okay." I don't know what the next facial thaw will bring. I suppose there's still a shell of "Golly, what's up next?" in there, but it's less eager for the answer. Suddenly Salad turns to Inevitably, Salad.

And it also occurs to me, I've never been to Ibiza.

But at least I did say "staff." Newspaper staff, and I was getting to spend the day at the best of all places, within the rarefied safety of a set, where I got to be one of the exquisite captives who don't have to think: The day is mapped, you eat what's given, you're fully preened, everything is safe and regularly cleaned by a fresh swirl of water, Eva Longoria loves children, everything you need is there, all kinds of oatmeal. Teas. All the poodles and otters and sweet German shepherds and seahorses and finches and egrets and others are all unmuzzled, unchained, uncaged, uninhibited, and singing. People are kind, and we are all just cooking light. This is the easiest way, and I'd be here all day.

Hi—

The Text gets one rounded scoop of dry food in the morning, (around 9— he might wake you up earlier, but just ignore him if you can) and one scant scoop plus half a can of wet food at night (9 pm). Please mix the dry and wet together a little or he'll just eat the wet and leave the dry.

Now, the cats might try to eat what the Text doesn't finish, and sometimes they'll even push him away, so you pretty much have to stand there and watch while they eat. When they seem like they're done, just take all the bowls away. Also— make sure the Text's bowl is on top of the dryer. That helps.

I filled the water well with water (Brita— in the fridge) but you need to keep an eye on it because some- times it gets dirty and you need to change it.

Also, if the Text sounds wheezy, you need to give him his medicine— it's in the cupboard where the food is. It's not too hard: just put some

241

in the dropper, hold the back of his head, and shove it up his ass. He might bite you, so do it fast, while petting him and saying "It's okay, it's okay." Give him a fish treat after. (Cupboard.)

Other than that, have fun! We'll be at the:
Colorado Belle Hotel & Casino
Laughlin, Nevada
(702) 298-4000
under the name "Mr. and Mrs. Thomas Cruise."
And we'll have our cells on us, but I don't know if we'll get reception:
Stacey (213) 590-7870
Kenny (323) 459-9355

In case of emergency:
Vet: (323) 461-3575
Poison Control: 1-800-222-1222

Thanks again! See you Monday!

(P.S.: Please, please, please take lemons! Our tree is overflowing!)

ACKNOWLEDGMENTS

My very warmest to Kenny, Mom, Dad, Christie Smith, the joy that is Brant Rumble, Daniel Greenberg, Lee, Sue, Cary, Joey, Tess, Gwyn, Samantha, Steven, Jennifer, Peter, Andrew, Claire, Jacks, Janet and Lonnie, Debbie, Mike, Samantha, Heidi Bauer, Sarah Cunningham, Benmont Tench, Richard Rushfield, Paul F. Tompkins, Jenny Hunter, Ant Hines (even if he hadn't asked), Peter Baynham, Tommi and Rob Zabrecky, Digby, Blanche, Elliott, Maxie, Joon, Olive, Kelly, Perry, Navin, Martha, David Granger, A. J. Jacobs, Ross MacLochness, Peter Martin (all of *Esquire*, really), David Bowie, and, I suppose, Iman.